CLASSIFIED FILES:

The Yellowing Pages

A Report on Scholars' Access to Government Documents
By Carol M. Barker and Matthew H. Fox

The Twentieth Century Fund/New York/1972

The Twentieth Century Fund, founded in 1919 and endowed by Edward A. Filene, devotes the major share of its resources to research, concentrating on objective and critical studies of institutions. It publishes the results of its research in report or book form. The Fund attempts to ensure the scholarly quality of books and reports appearing under its imprint; the Trustees and the staff, however, accord authors complete freedom in the statement of opinion and the interpretation of fact.

Library of Congress Catalog Card No. 72-80587
SBN 87078-127-8

Contents

The authors are research associates on the staff of The Twentieth Century Fund. Carol Barker received her doctorate in political science from Columbia University. Matthew Fox studied history at the University of Wisconsin and was a working journalist before coming to the Fund. In writing the report, the authors interviewed numerous government officials and met and corresponded with many diplomatic and military historians who have confronted the government's classification system in carrying out their research. The authors wish to thank Robert Barzilay who edited the manuscript. However, the authors take full responsibility for the facts, opinions and conclusions set forth here.

March 1972

Introduction

The United States has always been known for the relative openness with which it conducts its official business. This is entirely consistent with democratic theory, which calls for an informed citizenry able to evaluate the performance of its elected representatives. Openness is maintained by the various checks and balances of government, by congressional debate of public policy, by the fact that partisan administrations and politicians necessarily seek to win support for their programs, and by the alertness and vigilance of the press.

But there are areas of its business that government considers sacrosanct; and it is in these areas that conflicts arise between government and public over the issue of state secrecy. In the last quarter century, that issue has seemed to grow larger as government in one way or another has increasingly asserted a prerogative to classify its activities and its archives.

This trend has been a natural concomitant of the enlarged role of the United States in world affairs during and since World War II, and of the growing power and complexity of the federal government on the domestic scene. With the increased centralization of authority and responsibility in Washington, government bureaucracy has expanded, and each additional layer of officialdom has meant still another agency able to stamp "secret" or "confidential" on a record that may well merit neither. For American officials, like officials anywhere, are constrained, sometimes by reasons of state but often for self-protection or self-advancement, to classify a wide range of information; and it is here that the balance teeters between what can—or should—be made public and what is necessarily kept confidential.

In a recent article in *The New York Times Magazine,* Arthur Schlesinger, Jr., identified six categories of government operations where secrecy seemed essentially unassailable: (1) diplomatic negotiations; (2) intelligence activities; (3) warfare; (4) information that "might compromise foreign governments or leaders or American friends or agents in foreign lands"; (5) confidential data about individuals, e.g., internal revenue matters; (6) "official plans or decisions which, if prematurely disclosed, would lead to speculation in lands or commodities, pre-emptive buying, private enrichment and higher government costs."[1]

There is little argument about three of these categories. The American people have always accepted the need for secrecy in matters of national defense. Similarly, the public not only condones but advocates secrecy in matters involving the democratic guarantee of the right of privacy. It does not want to see anyone benefit unfairly from premature knowledge of government projects.

Nevertheless, the Pentagon Papers affair and the revelations by columnist Jack Anderson of the Nixon Administration's position in the India-Pakistan War have served to point up the ambivalence of the public about how much secrecy the government is entitled to maintain in matters of foreign policy. They have raised the question of the people's right to know about such policies, to have a voice in their formulation through its elected

[1] "The Secrecy Dilemma," *The New York Times Magazine,* February 6, 1972, p. 12.

representatives, and to pass judgment on the performance of the government and its officials.

Patently, many dealings with foreign governments would be impossible if carried on in public. Diplomacy in a goldfish bowl is an absurdity. But there is a grave question whether matters of war and peace should not be "tilted" by the weight of public opinion as well as by the judgment of government officials. The divisiveness aroused by the Vietnam War clearly indicates that the wishes of the people ought to be part of decision-making in a democracy where policy objectives presumably are based on the will of the people and effective policy depends on widespread public support.

There is even danger in excessive secrecy in intelligence activities that impinge on or interfere with foreign policy. The U-2 affair, exposing the government's effort to maintain secrecy about its surveillance procedures over the Soviet Union when secrecy was no longer possible, embarrassed the Eisenhower Administration in its foreign policy. Far more troubling are the instances, such as the Central Intelligence Agency's involvement in Laos, where intelligence agencies formulate and carry out foreign policy free from congressional or any other public control.

As a result of the American involvement in Vietnam and in other areas abroad since World War II, secrecy has more and more become suspect. Frequently, it is held to be deliberately obfuscating. As a result, politics no longer stops at the water's edge, and the public has become less and less willing to let foreign policy go unquestioned. It is here that the press in particular has an important role as mediator and arbiter of what is, or should be, publicly debatable.

Mr. Schlesinger has observed that "the functioning of democracy requires some rough but rational balance between secrecy and disclosure, between official control of information and public need for it." He cited Supreme Court Justice Potter Stewart's view that "secrecy can be preserved only when credibility is truly maintained." But when the proliferation of security classification gets out of hand, it invites defiance, which is part of the explanation for what happened in the case of the Pentagon Papers and Anderson's revelations.[2]

The focus of this paper, however, is not on secrecy involving day-to-day matters of public concern. It is on the interest of scholars and historians who must cope with the maze of security restrictions to gain access to government records and archives in order to evaluate and understand past policies and activities.

A scholar may act as a commentator on current affairs; but in doing so, he becomes a practitioner of the "in-depth" journalism that is so much in demand and so much needed. Our concern, though, is with the historian or political scientist engaged in the relatively long-range evaluation of policy where independent analysis and insight may offer judgments on past government performance and perhaps suggest some guidelines for future policy.

In this paper, therefore, we have attempted to avoid those issues that involve journalistic initiative or free-press guarantees. Rather, our intent has been to demonstrate how, why, and when the government maintains security over state papers and other records of its business and how its practices and procedures affect access to archives by those intent on scholarly research.

In essence, the security classification system and other restrictions on access to records permit government officials to control the flow of information to the public. The executive departments, particularly the presidency, can dominate the headlines with official pronouncements, news releases, press conferences, and publication of documents. An administration can even "blow the lid" on its own secrecy, as shown by President Nixon's recent disclosure of the secret negotiations with the North Vietnamese. Off-the-record briefings and leaks to the press permit officials to discuss policy and events—often without taking responsibility for what they reveal. Former officials publish memoirs of their years in office; government departments issue their own histories of significant events; favored scholars and journalists are sometimes given access to official records that remain off limits to others.

In each case, officials or former officials exercise discretion in

[2] *Ibid.*, p. 38.

choosing what to reveal and what to conceal. As a consequence, the public must rely on sources that have some vested interest in the information that is given out.

What the public has not received—or has waited decades for—are accounts of government operations based on firsthand records and commentaries by detached observers. The State Department, which has maintained a thirty-year limit on classification of its files, did not make the official record of American diplomacy in World War II available to the general public until January 1972. The documents on most of our cold-war diplomacy remain in closed files. The Joint Chiefs of Staff have only recently opened segments of their World War II records, and their postwar files are unavailable for any nonofficial purpose. Few Army records from the post-1945 period are available to unofficial researchers even on a restricted basis. Researchers at the Truman Library in Independence, Missouri, still cannot use some of the secret documents on which Mr. Truman based his memoirs, published in 1958.

In the last several years, scholars—both historians and political scientists—interested in the study and analysis of contemporary foreign policy and recent diplomatic history have protested the government's restrictions on study and research of official records.

Political controversy over secrecy and classification prompted President Nixon to issue on March 8 a comprehensive new directive, an executive order on Classification and Declassification of National Security Information. He signed his order, which superseded the system established by President Eisenhower, as the House Armed Services Committee and the Foreign Operations and Government Information Subcommittee were holding hearings on government secrecy, and the Senate had before it a bill introduced by Senator Edmund Muskie entitled the "Truth in Government Act of 1971." The new order provides needed reforms, but the structure of the Nixon system is similar to its predecessor, which means that its success will depend heavily on the good intentions of those who carry it out.

What is significant is that Nixon has kept the classification ball in his court, preserving executive prerogative and taking the edge off the congressional hearings and pending legislation. Whether his efforts will satisfy the scholarly community is doubtful, as its experience with other attempted reforms has resulted in widespread skepticism. We propose to deal with the validity—or lack of it—of its grievances. This paper investigates the problems involved in independent research in diplomatic and military archives, the distortions that may result from unequal and privileged access to government records, and proposals for reform of the classification system, including Nixon's new order.

Scholars concerned with the problems of access and officials charged with administering research programs have been consulted. The official regulations covering secrecy and declassification have been studied and case histories cited.

While it is recognized that there is a need for secrecy in many aspects of the conduct of government business, especially in the fields of foreign affairs and defense, it is also clear that some balance must be struck between that necessity and the need for public disclosure. Justice Stewart's warning that excessive secrecy jeopardizes credibility has a corollary: The longer secrecy is maintained, the dimmer becomes the possibility of restoring credibility. It is through the archives of government that credibility and balance can be sought. Those archives are the target of the scholar, for if the past is to be any guide for the future, it must be an open past. The security classification system, as we see it, has kept it closed too long. President Nixon's new executive order on classification is a step in the right direction, and we look forward to the implementation of its reforms. For the words of Shakespeare, inscribed on the facade of the National Archives Building in Washington, are very much to the point: "What's past is prologue."

Chapter I
How Security Grew

Neither secrecy nor disclosure is mentioned in the United States Constitution. Protection of official records, derived originally from the "housekeeping" function of government, has been extended to embrace the secrecy of records. The security classification system was established by executive order rather than legislation and, over the years, just grew. In the past, Congress agreed to approve legislation sanctioning executive secrecy. Yet it sought to limit executive power by the passage of the Freedom of Information Act of 1966 (FOI), although the law failed to break down the barriers surrounding national security information. Since the Pentagon Papers affair, Congress for the first time has been considering legislative reform of the security classification system itself. By issuing his executive order, President Nixon forestalled such legislation, at least temporarily, preserving the tradition of an executive prerogative in national security matters.

From the beginning, the executive branch has justified withholding information on grounds of executive privilege, based on the constitutional separation of powers and the President's responsibility to "take care that the laws be faithfully executed."

The privilege[1] has been invoked time and again, from the administration of George Washington to the administration of Richard Nixon.

Executive privilege was first cited in 1796 after Congress requested documents relating to General St. Clair's ill-fated expedition against the Indians. After establishing his authority to withhold information, President Washington acceded to the congressional request, although later he claimed the privilege in refusing to transmit to Congress the records concerning the negotiation of the Jay Treaty. This privilege has been used three times by President Nixon: once to protect information in FBI files; a second time, in August 1971, to reject a Senate Foreign Relations Committee request for a copy of the Pentagon's five-year military assistance plan, and the third, in March 1972, to withhold a State Department report on American aid to Cambodia from the House Government Information Subcommittee.

In refusing the Foreign Relations Committee's request for what he described as "internal working documents," President Nixon argued that "unless privacy of preliminary exchange of views between personnel of the executive branch can be maintained, the full, frank and healthy exchange of opinion which is essential for the successful administration of government would be muted."[2]

From President Washington to Nixon, the concept of executive privilege, which has been so vaguely defined that it can be made to fit almost any circumstance, has most often been used to deny Congress access to the internal proceedings of the executive branch. For example, when President Eisenhower, in 1954, forbade the employees of the Department of the Army to testify about any intradepartmental discussions concerning the Army-McCarthy dispute, Congress found that the order was being used by nineteen other executive agencies to protect their own internal proceedings. Congressional criticism over the years has successively persuaded Presidents Kennedy, Johnson, and Nixon to reserve

[1] On executive privilege, see Francis Rourke, *Secrecy and Publicity: Dilemmas of Democracy* (Baltimore, Johns Hopkins Press, 1961), pp. 64–74.

[2] *The New York Times*, September 1, 1971; March 17, 1972.

the privilege for the President alone, and then only in special circumstances.

Executive secrecy also has been bolstered by statute. In 1960, the House Subcommittee on Foreign Operations and Government Information discovered 172 statutes permitting nondisclosure of information in specific instances and only 75 statutes requiring disclosure. The executive departments in general have justified withholding information from the public by relying on a broad interpretation of three pieces of legislation designed, for the most part, to limit executive secrecy.

The Housekeeping Act of 1789, for example, authorized department heads to provide for "the custody, use and preservation of . . . [a department's] records, papers and property appertaining to it." In 1958, Congress amended this act to make it clear that it "does not authorize withholding information from the public or limiting the availability of records to the public." But the amendment failed to limit the executive's discretionary power to protect information.[3]

Earlier the Administrative Procedure Act of 1946 had attempted to establish the principle that "administrative operations and procedures are public property which the general public . . . is entitled to know." Although requiring publication of information relating to the organization, powers, and procedures of the executive agencies, the legislation exempted matters of purely internal management and limited access to agency records to persons "properly and directly concerned." Even in such cases, agencies could decide against disclosure "in the public interest" or for "good cause." Not surprisingly, the executive departments came to rely on the Administrative Procedure Act to justify the withholding rather than the publication of information.[4]

The Freedom of Information Act of 1966 (FOI) represents the third and latest congressional effort to limit the assumption of executive authority to withhold information from the public. The legislation, which amends the Administrative Procedure Act

[3] Rourke, *Secrecy and Publicity*, pp. 47–48, 59–60.
[4] *Ibid.*, pp. 57–58; Joan M. Katz, "The Games Bureaucrats Play: Hide and Seek Under the Freedom of Information Act," *The Texas Law Review* 48 (1970), p. 1261.

of 1946, makes disclosure of information to "any person" and equal access to agency records the general rule, while placing the burden of proof for nondisclosure on the government. Consisting of four provisions for disclosing information and nine exemptions from disclosure, it mandates the publication in the Federal Register of agency organization, procedures and general rules and provides that agency opinions, orders, records and proceedings be available for public inspection. The nine exemptions from these disclosure provisions cover records relating to national defense and foreign policy protected by executive order; internal personnel rules and practices; records specifically exempt by statute; trade secrets and privileged or confidential commercial and financial information; inter- and intra-agency communications; personnel and medical files; investigatory files compiled for law enforcement purposes; records relating to regulation or supervision of financial institutions; geological and geophysical information concerning wells, i.e., oil or gas. In the event that an agency bars disclosure, the citizen requesting records can seek injunctive relief in the courts.[5]

Although the nine exemptions are not obligatory—they allow, but do not require, withholding records—critics claim that the exemptions are so broad that the government has lost very little of its discretionary power.[6] In particular, the FOI Act has done little if anything to facilitate access to foreign policy or defense information or to curb excessive secrecy in these particular areas. One legal analyst has argued that the FOI Act serves to reinforce secrecy in national security matters by giving statutory endorsement to the executive's claim of privilege to withhold information.[7]

[5] United States Code, Title 5, Section 552; see also U.S. Department of Justice, "Attorney General's Memorandum on the Public Information Section of the Administrative Procedure Act," June 1967.

[6] Katz, "Games Bureaucrats Play," p. 1262; Kenneth Culp Davis, "The Information Act: A Preliminary Analysis," *The University of Chicago Law Review* 34 (1967), p. 803; Ralph Nader, et al., "A Status Report on the Responsiveness of Some Federal Agencies to the People's Right to Know about Their Government," August 26, 1969, reprinted in the *Congressional Record*, House, September 3, 1969, pp. 24073–77; John H. Rothchild, "Finding the Facts Bureaucrats Hide," *The Washington Monthly* (January 1972) pp. 15–27, criticizes the exemptions, but finds that determined use of provisions of the FOI Act can bring results.

[7] Davis, "The Information Act," pp. 784–85.

Apart from executive and statutory provisions, which apply to all sorts of official records, military and diplomatic information has traditionally been privileged under common law. Until relatively recently, the public took it for granted that foreign and defense policies were areas of government expertise that, in keeping with the revered tradition of "my country, right or wrong," rarely came under question. Nevertheless, special provisions were established for both censorship and security during wartime, when secrecy took on special significance. It was only after World War II that the security system imposed by the exigencies of war was carried over for the first time into peacetime, largely because of the turnabout in relations with the Soviet Union, a fighting ally against Germany, Italy and Japan. This cold-war period brought an increase in loyalty, security, and classification programs, and intensification of emphasis on security put the spotlight on both breaches of and challenges to official secrecy. Opponents of the Soviet Union, particularly some right-wing legislators, clamored for disclosure of foreign policy secrets, which they believed would reveal serious mistakes by the Roosevelt and Truman administrations. During the 1950s, there were the Senate investigations— particularly the Army-McCarthy hearings—resulting from the late Senator Joseph R. McCarthy's charges that government officials had aided and abetted Soviet—and Communist Chinese—designs. Still later, during the 1960s, left-wing elements and members of the peace movement condemned excessive secrecy and, like earlier partisans, wanted access to foreign policy files. Just within the last year, with the release of the Anderson and Pentagon Papers, the security classification system itself has become a target of public criticism.

Security Classification: The Postwar System

Three Presidents before Nixon—Truman, Eisenhower, and Kennedy—tried to set up machinery designed to protect sensitive papers. Each of them recognized that the security system was needed but could get out of hand. Their efforts contrasted with the rather cavalier attitude prevailing before World War II, when secrecy restrictions in the State Department and the military establishment were by and large erratic and lax. Recalling the way things were then handled, former ambassador Robert Murphy has observed: "There had been practically no security precautions in the State Department prior to the war. Suddenly we had too much. Every report seemed to contain secrets; the most innocuous information was 'classified'; a swollen staff of security agents hampered the work of everybody."[8]

At the end of the war, when general censorship ended, the Departments of State and Defense continued to use a four-grade classification system: top secret, secret, confidential, and restricted. The objective was to prevent dissemination of sensitive information, but much of this classification seemed to be either superfluous or inadequate. For example, President Truman cited a confidential study of censorship breaches by Yale University, which reported that 95 percent of all secret government information was being published in the press.[9]

In response to such reports, President Truman, on the advice of the National Security Council, issued Executive Order 10290 on September 24, 1951. The Truman order authorized all executive agencies, civilian as well as military, to safeguard documents, "the authorized disclosure of which would or could harm, tend to impair, or otherwise threaten the security of the nation. . . ."[10] Under the order, all agencies were instructed to make use of the four-tiered classification system employed by the Departments of State and Defense. Each agency head was granted the authority to delegate responsibility for classifying secret material. However, the standards for classification and the procedures for declassification were quite vague.[11]

Executive Order 10290 proved extremely unpopular, particularly with the press. The American Society of Newspaper Editors

[8] James Russell Wiggins, *Freedom or Secrecy*, revised ed. (New York, Oxford University Press, 1964), p. 99; Murphy, *Diplomat Among Warriors* (New York, Doubleday & Sons, Inc., 1964), p. 452.

[9] *The New York Times*, October 5, 1951, p. 12.

[10] Code of Federal Regulations, Title 3, *The President*, Chapter II, Executive Orders (1949–1953 Compilation), p. 789.

[11] *Ibid.*, pp. 789–797.

and the AP Managing Editors Association attacked it, charging that it would allow officials to cover up blunders and politically motivated projects under the guise of national security. The press also claimed the directive would permit officials to leak whatever confidential material they wished.[12] A *New York Times* editorial summarized much of the press criticism:

> [It is] . . . broad in its powers but vague in its definitions. . . . Vast discretion is placed in the hands of a large number of officials with no check upon how that discretion is exercised. The result is that the effect of this order will depend on a considerable number of very fallible human judgments.[13]

President Eisenhower took account of such criticisms by issuing on November 5, 1953, Executive Order 10501, dealing with security classification. Eisenhower's order, though amended, remained in effect for twenty years and is the basic security classification order—"the bible of security stamping," according to former Pentagon aide William G. Florence. It limited the number of agencies with authority to classify information, further restricted the number of agency heads who could delegate the authority to classify, eliminated the "restricted" category of security, and defined a more elaborate system for declassification.

Executive Order 10501 defined three levels of classification.[14] The most stringent label was "Top Secret." It was to be applied

> only to that information or material the defense aspect of which is paramount, and the unauthorized disclosure of which could result in exceptionally grave damage to the nation such as leading to a definite break in diplomatic relations affecting the defense of the United States, an armed attack against the United States or its allies, a war, or the compromise of military or defense plans, or intelligence operations, or scientific or technological developments vital to the national defense.[15]

---

[12] *The New York Times,* September 30, 1951, Section IV, pp. 2, 10.

[13] *The New York Times,* September 28, 1951, p. 30.

[14] Code of Federal Regulations, Title 3, *The President,* Chapter II, Executive Orders (1949–1953 Compilation), pp. 979–86.

[15] *Ibid.,* p. 979.

The "Secret" label was to be applied to a document when disclosure could result in

> serious damage to the nation, such as by jeopardizing the international relations of the United States, endangering the effectiveness of a program or policy of vital importance to the national defense, or compromising important military or defense plans, scientific or technological developments important to national defense, or information revealing important intelligence operations.[16]

"Confidential," the least stringent and also the vaguest classification, applied to unauthorized disclosure "which could be prejudicial to the defense interest of the nation."[17]

The vagueness of all of these definitions left great leeway for the overly cautious classifier. The Eisenhower order also tried to combat excessive classification by restricting the number of people with the authority to classify. It limited the number of agencies with full classifying authority to twenty-eight (the number climbed back to thirty-eight). In these thirty-eight agencies—from the White House to the Department of Labor—the agency head could delegate his authority to subordinates although the delegation "shall be limited as severely as is consistent with the orderly and expeditious transaction of government business." In thirteen agencies not directly involved in foreign affairs or defense—the Post Office and the Tennessee Valley Authority, for example—only the agency head had the authority to classify records.[18]

Because the sensitivity of national security information is likely to decrease over time, the Eisenhower order provided procedures for downgrading and declassifying previously classified material. Each agency with classification authority was to designate officials responsible for continuous review of such documents. "Formal procedures" for review were to be established "to preserve the effectiveness and the integrity of the classification system and to eliminate accumulation of classified material that no longer requires protection in the defense interest." The official classifying

[16] *Ibid.*, pp. 979–80.
[17] *Ibid.*, p. 980.
[18] *Ibid.*

a document was required "to the fullest extent possible" to indicate the time or conditions under which the document could be declassified without formal review. When automatic declassification was not possible, declassification required the consent of the original classifying authority.[19]

These directives, however well-intended, proved to be ineffective in accelerating the declassification process. To remedy the situation, the executive order was amended by President Kennedy in 1961 to include more specific guidelines for automatic downgrading and declassification. The new amendment, Executive Order 10964, exempted three categories from automatic declassification. Only documents not falling into these three categories were declared subject to automatic downgrading at three-year intervals and declassification after twelve years. These procedures for automatic declassification, which applied primarily to the Defense Department, were seldom implemented.[20] Instead, classified documents had to be examined page by page by an official in the originating office before clearance was granted. Declassification ranked low among the priorities of government bureaus. As a result, in the absence of outside pressure, most records once classified remain classified. According to President Nixon, the National Archives now has in its possession an estimated 160 million pages of classified documents dating from the start of World War II and over 300 million pages dating from 1946 to 1954. These figures do not include the millions of more recent records locked in departmental files. The declassification of the World War II documents alone is expected to cost $6 million and take five years to carry out. The General Accounting Office estimates the annual cost of administering the security classification system at $60 to $80 million.[21]

So much has been classified and so little declassified since World War II that even the government itself has been compelled

<hr />

[19] *Ibid.*, pp. 980–81.

[20] James McCartney, "What Should Be Secret?" *Columbia Journalism Review*, September–October 1971, p. 43.

[21] *The New York Times*, August 4, 1971; January 24, 1972; press statement of President Nixon, March 8, 1972, in conjunction with the signing of the Executive Order on security classification.

to find ways of circumventing the rules by either leaking classified information to newsmen or including such material in public statements. The government also devised legal means for granting limited public access to classified material.

President Eisenhower's Executive Order 10501 originally restricted use of classified information "to persons whose official duties require such access in the interest of promoting national defense and only if they have been determined to be trustworthy."[22] In 1959, Eisenhower amended this provision in Executive Order 10816 to provide for nonofficial historical research in classified materials. Executive Order 10816 reads:

> As an exception to the standard for access prescribed in the first sentence of section 7, but subject to all other provisions of this order, the head of an agency may permit persons outside the executive branch performing functions in connection with historical research projects to have access to classified defense information originated within his agency if he determines that: (a) access to the information will be clearly consistent with the interests of national defense, and, (b) the person to be granted access is trustworthy: Provided, that the head of the agency shall take appropriate steps to assure that classified information is not published or otherwise compromised.[23]

President Eisenhower was evidently motivated to issue the order by the desire of the late Secretary of State John Foster Dulles to permit scholars to use the microfilmed copies of official Dulles papers deposited at the Princeton Library.[24] The order was promulgated shortly before Dulles's death. Philip A. Crowl, now chairman of the history department at the University of Nebraska, claims that Dulles's wish for the earliest possible scholarly access to his documents, "certainly well before the entirety of State Department documents were made completely accessible," has been subverted by the extension to these microfilms of the

---

[22] Code of Federal Regulations, Title 3, Chapter II (1949–1953 Compilation), p. 983.

[23] Executive Order 10816, Code of Federal Regulations, Title III, *The President,* Chapter II, Executive Orders (1959–1963 Compilation), pp. 351–52.

[24] *The New York Times,* May 5, 1959, p. 19; May 17, 1959, p. 72.

State Department's lengthy (now twenty-six-year) embargo on nonofficial access to its records.[25]

The Freedom of Information Act
and Classified Documents

The Freedom of Information Act attempted to provide another avenue for private citizens seeking access to classified documents. Although the first of the nine exemptions to the law applies to matters "specifically required by executive order to be kept secret in the interest of the national defense or foreign policy," an executive agency can use its discretion to declassify individual, identifiable (i.e., specific) security-classified documents requested by a private citizen. If the agency refuses such requests the applicant can take his case to a U.S. district court.

In the first case in which that exemption faced judicial review, the courts refused to challenge the government's decision. In 1967, Julius Epstein, a historian at the Hoover Institution on Revolution, War and Peace at Stanford University, sued the Secretary of the Army for refusing to release a top secret file of Anglo-American documents on the forced repatriation of anti-Communist Russian prisoners of war after World War II. The Army insisted that the documents, dating from 1946 and 1947, could not be declassified under the provisions of Executive Order 10501. Mr. Epstein argued that the FOI Act gave the courts authority to judge whether or not records are "improperly withheld" on the basis of the first exemption to the FOI Act. He asked the court to examine the records *in camera* to determine whether or not they were properly classified under the executive order and therefore exempt from disclosure. Epstein's position was supported by an affidavit from Congressman John E. Moss (D.—California), former chairman of the House Government Information Subcommittee, which drafted the FOI Act. But the U.S. District Court for the Northern District of California and the U.S. Court of Appeals for the Ninth Circuit both refused to subpoena the documents. They ruled that on the basis of the

[25] Letter from Crowl, February 4, 1971.

description of the documents alone classification was neither "arbitrary" nor "capricious" and was therefore proper under the FOI Act. The Court of Appeals found that "the function of determining whether secrecy is required in the national interest is expressly assigned to the executive. The judicial inquiry is limited to the question whether an appropriate Executive Order has been made as to the material in question . . . the question of what is desirable in the interest of national defense and foreign policy is not the sort of question that courts are designed to deal with."[26] The Supreme Court denied Epstein's petition for a writ of certiorari. He concluded from his experience that judicial review is meaningless without judicial examination of the documents in question.

Two members of the House Government Information Subcommittee, Moss and Ogden R. Reid, Democrat from New York, experienced a similar rebuff when they tried to make use of the FOI Act to seek judicial review of the Nixon Administration's decision to withhold certain portions of the celebrated Pentagon history of the war in Vietnam from the government's edition of the Pentagon Papers. Judge Gerhard A. Gesell of the Federal District Court of the District of Columbia refused to review the documents in question, arguing that the first exemption eliminated the need for independent judicial review of executive decisions in matters of national security, a responsibility, he observed, for which judges are ill-equipped in any case.

Congressman Reid responded to the decision by calling for new legislation creating an independent reviewing body to evaluate classification decisions and to order declassification.[27] In urging new legislation, he called for automatic declassification and congressional oversight and also suggested that Congress reserve the right to publish material "improperly classified by the executive contrary to statute when its classification is not a matter of national security and is simply a device to avoid governmental embarrassment." He proposed that Congress "come to

---

[26] *Congressional Record* (House), October 14, 1970, p. H10177.
[27] *The New York Times*, December 8, 1971.

grips with executive privilege" in order to put an end to the "collision between the executive and Congress that has been going on since George Washington assumed office."[28]

Nixon's Executive Order

President Nixon—who waited until after the Pentagon Papers were published to announce the existence of an interagency committee to evaluate the classification system—signed a new executive order on March 8, 1972, that he described as a measure "to lift the veil of secrecy which now enshrouds altogether too many papers written by employees of the federal establishment—and to do so without jeopardizing any of our legitimate defense or foreign policy interests."[29] The order, which becomes effective June 1, 1972, and incorporates access and security classification regulations from previous executive orders, the State Department, and the presidential libraries system, appears more political than potent.[30]

On the surface, it treats many of the basic criticisms of the classification system. Nixon termed it a "more progressive system" than Eisenhower's Executive Order 10501 promulgated in 1953, and there is no doubt that it contains strong language for limiting secrecy and for allowing the public greater access to the operations and actions of government. However, citizens who think they may become privy to a greater portion of government operations or scholars who believe they will gain access to a larger number of formerly top secret files, and Congress, which might conclude that hitherto secret operations of the executive will now be opened to it, may all be disappointed. The Nixon Executive Order on Classification and Declassification of National Security Information and Material will still rest on administrative interpretation and most likely will prove unable (as was the Eisen-

[28] *The New York Times*, July 13, 1971, p. 37.

[29] Press statement of President Nixon, March 8, 1972, at signing of executive order.

[30] All references in this section to President Nixon's Executive Order 11652 on Classification and Declassification of National Security Information and Material are taken from a mimeographed copy released March 8, 1972, at the signing of the order.

hower order) to move an appreciable number of diplomatic, military, and foreign policy-related records into the public arena.

The new order reduces the number of agencies and persons who have the authority to impose top secret stamps. This reduction— from thirty-eight to twelve agencies and from 5,100 to 1,860 top secret classifiers—should reduce the number of records classified (an additional thirteen agencies retain the authority to use the secret and confidential labels). Moreover, all officials granted classifying authority must be identified in writing.

In addition, the Nixon order for the first time brings the presidential libraries under the rubric of the classification system. The new provision, however, only formalizes the existing regulations (see Chapter III).

There are three classification categories in the Nixon order— Top Secret, Secret, and Confidential—all strictly applied to information concerning the national defense or foreign relations of the United States and following the language of previous executive orders. "Top secret" describes material that requires "the highest degree of protection" and classifies information that if disclosed "could reasonably be expected to cause exceptionally grave damage to the national security." The regulation promises that this classification "shall be used with the utmost restraint."

The "Secret" label identifies material that requires a "substantial degree of protection" and if disclosed could "reasonably be expected to cause serious damage to the national security." It is to be "sparingly used." "Confidential" information must be protected when its disclosure could cause damage to national security.

The caution that Nixon urges upon those who will use these classifications was also expressed by President Eisenhower in 1953 when he charged that "unnecessary classification and over-classification shall be scrupulously avoided."[31] Nixon went further by asserting that no information shall be "classified in order to conceal inefficiency or administrative error, to prevent embarrass-

[31] Code of Federal Regulations, Title 3, Chapter II (1949–1953 Compilation), p. 980.

ment to a person or department, to restrain competition or independent initiatives, or to prevent for any reason the release of information which does not require protection in the interest of national security." But these commendable ideals depend on the good intentions of those involved in classification, which have been one of the weak links in previous attempts to limit secrecy and increase access.

Although top secret material in general will be downgraded to secret after the second year, to confidential after the fourth year, and declassified and deposited in public archives after the tenth—the Kennedy amendment to the Eisenhower order authorized a twelve-year declassification schedule—information classified after May 31, 1972, which discloses a "system, plan, installation, project or specific foreign relations matter the continuing protection of which is essential to the national security" will be exempted from the ten-year declassification rule. So will information furnished in confidence by a foreign government and classified information covered by statute or pertaining to intelligence matters or which would place a person in "immediate jeopardy." The Kennedy amendment, attacked by critics as unworkable, also exempted from declassification information that was extremely sensitive or material that warranted "some degree of classification for an indefinite period."

Despite the similarity of the old and new orders, the new Nixon measure gives somewhat greater emphasis to declassification. (Kennedy established four categories for declassifying documents, three of which were exempt from automatic declassification; Nixon has created two categories: material that can be declassified after ten years and material that cannot because it falls under one of four exemptions.) But while Nixon's order urges exemptions be "kept to the absolute minimum consistent with national security requirements," it still leaves plenty of leeway for individual interpretation of what material requires national security protection.

A new section added to the executive order calls for the declassification after 30 years of all documents previously exempted from automatic declassification, a practice already followed by the State Department. However, the head of any department can prolong the secrecy of a document for "national security" reasons without limitation. If the records were classified under Eisenhower's executive order, the Archivist of the United States is responsible for reviewing classification after thirty years.

The most disappointing aspect of the Nixon order is the provision for review of classification decisions. Citizens can request a formal review by the classifying department but only of documents classified beyond the ten-year limit. (The FOI Act, in contrast, provides for review at any time.) Furthermore, request for review must specify the document "with sufficient particularity to enable the department to identify it" so that it can be retrieved "with only a reasonable amount of effort." These requirements are not materially different from those established under the FOI Act but omit the Act's provisions for judicial appeal. The department thus preserves complete discretion to reject declassification, subject only to its own formal review. To be sure, the burden of proof for keeping records classified longer than ten years rests with the government; but it is the classifiers themselves who are asked to sit in judgment on their own decisions.

The scholar, moreover, does not work with individual documents. He needs to leaf through files examining the whole documentary record pertaining to the events he is studying. Who, except those on the inside, will know about the existence of specific classified documents? The new review procedures consequently will not be of much assistance to the scholar. Section Twelve of the new regulation, superseding Executive Order 10816, authorizes access to classified files for persons engaged in historical research or who have previously occupied policy-making positions to which they were appointed by the President. Such access, however, must not jeopardize national security interests or lead to publication or compromising of classified material.

It is unclear whether special access to classified files is permitted at any time after the issuing of a document or only at some point after the ten-year period. Under the new order, according to David Young, Special Assistant to the National Security Council, individual departments will retain the responsibility for setting up historical access programs as they have done under Executive Order 10816. Thus, scholars may still have to wait until after the publication of the *Foreign Relations of the United States* volumes for a given year before they can apply for access to State Department files. One conclusion that can be drawn from this vague section in a document which elsewhere strives for precision is that the Nixon Administration did not attach much significance to the problem of scholarly access. The important questions raised by the historical community about the twenty-six-year delay in seeing the documentary record and the debate about former officials and selected authors being privy to material closed to others are not dealt with in Nixon's order, and the problems they create will most likely continue.

Nixon has directed the Secretary of State to accelerate publication of the *Foreign Relations* documentary history series to reduce the time period before its publication from twenty-seven to twenty years, providing scholars and researchers with somewhat quicker access to State Department records. But both the order and comments from the State Department historical office indicate that documents classified prior to May 31, 1972, relating to foreign policy and diplomatic issues, will hardly be affected by Nixon's executive order. Except for those scheduled for automatic declassification after twelve years, these records will be declassified only after individual review or by action of the national archivist after thirty years.

A final major change is the creation of a watchdog committee to review the implementation of the order. It is to be composed of representatives from the Departments of State, Defense, and Justice, the Atomic Energy Commission, the Central Intelligence Agency and the National Security Council, with the chairman appointed by the President. In proposing the committee, Nixon broadened the existing Eisenhower order that called for the President to "designate a member of his staff who shall receive, consider, and take action upon suggestions or complaints from nongovernment sources relating to the operations of this order." In addition, under the Nixon system, as under the Eisenhower, the National Security Council is mandated to monitor the implementation of the order.

The Eisenhower directive failed to insure public access and rapid declassification of government information. Neither did it cut the flow of leaks of classified material to press and partisan publicists. The Nixon order has more teeth, providing sanctions for both overclassification and leakage: The overly zealous stamper will receive an "administrative reprimand"; the government employee who is found responsible for the unauthorized release or disclosure of national security information will be subject to "prompt and stringent administrative action" and possible criminal prosecution. But its substantive reforms are few and dependent on the good will of the officials responsible for interpreting and enforcing them.

The fact is that the security classification system as it exists today has evolved from a rather simple device for executive control over sensitive records to a complicated bureaucratic machine with a life of its own. Failure of legislative restraints and the malfunctioning of the system itself have caused widespread dissatisfaction and distrust—in Congress, in the press and among the public. All feel deprived of information essential for participation in the policy-making process. The scholar especially sees himself cut off from access to records without which study and appraisal of policy are impossible. Except for privileged access in certain cases, this lack of access seems to be largely true when the classification system is examined in the light of executive departmental regulations.

Chapter II
How the System Works

It is only through examination of the government's classification system as it is variously implemented by different federal departments that the extent of its hindrances to scholars can be appreciated. Under the broad authority of Executive Orders 10501 and 10816 and the FOI Act, each executive department or agency involved in foreign policy and defense established its own procedures for making its records available to the public and for authorizing nonofficial search of official documents.

Because the procedures for use of classified records vary from department to department, the potential researcher must decipher a welter of regulations, ranging from the no-access rule of the Joint Chiefs of Staff and the Central Intelligence Agency to the State Department's policy of automatic declassification after thirty years. Despite their differences, the regulations present similar problems for nonofficial researchers. All of the agencies involved in foreign policy and national security affairs produce quantities of classified documents. Clearance requirements for individuals and subsequent review of notes and manuscripts make research at best inconvenient. Access is further—even critically—limited by the fact that officials enjoy a large degree of discretion in the application of declassification and access rules. This discretion can lead to an overcautious interpretation of rules and makes possible unequal treatment of individual researchers, which in turn invites distrust between scholars and archivists. The Nixon order is unlikely to alter this state of affairs.

The State Department

The State Department's regular publication of American foreign policy documents and its thirty-year rule for opening its archives have made it the most open and public foreign office of any major world power. However, Dr. William Franklin, director of the State Department's Historical Office, reports that Great Britain, Canada, and Australia are now also following a thirty-year rule in opening their World War II records. He believes their action is helpful to the American declassification program because the State Department cannot disclose records involving foreign powers without their permission—a policy that slows down declassification of documents dealing with foreign affairs.

According to Franklin, France is contemplating a thirty-year rule that "may" be implemented in 1976. But he notes that most countries have a fifty-year rule or longer, and some have no set patterns of disclosure because "they do not want to admit to not having a specific program."[1] Arthur Schlesinger, Jr., has reported one instance in which Italy barred access to records that were 110 years old, representing in his view, "an excess of caution."[2] Franklin believes the opening of now-classified State Department records should be linked to the disclosure policies of other nations. Because it is not known what percentage of department records must be withheld because of the potential reactions of foreign powers, there also is no way of knowing the quality—or quantity —of currently classified documents that might be made available if other nations liberalized their rules.

[1] Conversation with Franklin, February 8, 1972.
[2] "The Secrecy Dilemma," *The New York Times Magazine*, February 6, 1972, p. 43.

The pride of the State Department's historical program is its compilation of American foreign policy documents, *Foreign Relations of the United States (FRUS)*. Although the State Department is years ahead of any of its foreign counterparts in the publication of its documentary history, the *FRUS* volumes today appear twenty-six years after the events they record. Because nonofficial researchers cannot gain access to State Department archives for a given year until after the publication of the *FRUS* volumes for that year, the diplomatic historian must wait a quarter of a century before he can study the documentary record of American foreign policy. Frustrated and impatient scholars are pressing for accelerated publication of the *FRUS* series or revision of the regulations to permit earlier prepublication access. Nixon's order makes no specific provisions for historical access prior to the publication of *FRUS* and leaves access for research purposes up to the individual departments. However, Nixon has ordered the State Department to cut the time lag in publishing the series from twenty-six to twenty years within the next three years. Ten years ago Secretary of State Dean Rusk also ordered publication after twenty years, to no avail.

Until 1972, State Department regulations provided for three stages of access to American foreign policy records. In the first stage—the closed period—department files for a given year were off limits to all unofficial researchers, although individual records could be obtained under the FOI Act. This so-called closed period in effect permitted virtually no access at all. The second stage—the restricted period—began with the publication of the FRUS volumes for a given year; during the restricted period, access was limited to scholars qualified to use classified documents under the provisions of Executive Order 10816. The third stage—the open period—began after thirty years with the automatic declassification of all security-classified records and their transfer to the National Archives, where they were opened to the public.

Because three of the eleven *FRUS* volumes for 1946 were still unpublished in early 1972, the State Department files from 1946 to the present were unavailable to the public. In January 1972, the department announced that its files for the years 1942–1945 had been opened for public use in the National Archives. This action beat the thirty-year rule by three years and in effect eliminated the period of restricted access.

The *FRUS* series is the government's major publication of recent official records. As such it is a valuable reference work and guide for research in American foreign policy. The difficulties that beset the publication of *FRUS* serve to illustrate many of the obstacles to nongovernmental use of recent official records.

The *FRUS* series began in 1861 when President Lincoln supplemented his annual address to Congress with a collection of foreign policy documents from the preceding year. From 1861 to 1906, the annual compilations of diplomatic correspondence usually appeared in the year following the events covered. This extraordinary procedure attracted little attention at home or abroad when the United States was regarded as a small power on the periphery of the European-dominated world. Nor did anybody seem much concerned about the effect of publicity on the conduct of current foreign policy.

Until the 1920s, the compilation of the *FRUS* volumes was usually a one-man job of uneven quality. But after World War I, the publication of American diplomatic documents became a more serious undertaking. In 1925, Secretary of State Frank B. Kellogg established the principles for systematic publication of documents that, with slight alterations, govern the *Foreign Relations* series to this day.[3]

The departmental regulations, printed in the preface to each *FRUS* volume, define the scope of the publication:

> The publication Foreign Relations of the United States constitutes the official record of the foreign policy of the United States. These volumes include, subject to necessary security considerations, all documents needed to give a comprehensive record of the major foreign policy decisions within the range of the Department of State's responsibilities, together with appropriate

[3] Richard W. Leopold, "The *Foreign Relations* Series: A Centennial Estimate," *The Mississippi Valley Historical Review* (March 1963), pp. 595–600; William M. Franklin, "The Future of the 'Foreign Relations' Series," *Department of State Bulletin* (September 15, 1969), p. 247.

materials concerning the facts which contributed to the formulation of policies. When further material is needed to supplement the documentation in the Department's files for a proper understanding of the relevant policies of the United States, such papers should be obtained from other Government agencies.

The regulations also define the standards of historical objectivity applied in the compilation of the documents:

There may be no alteration of the text, no deletions without indicating where in the text the deletion is made, and no omission of facts which were of major importance in reaching a decision. Nothing may be omitted for the purpose of concealing or glossing over what might be regarded by some as a defect of policy. However, certain omissions of documents are permissible for the following reasons:

    a. To avoid publication of matters which would tend to impede current diplomatic negotiations or other business.

    b. To condense the record and avoid repetition of needless details.

    c. To preserve the confidence reposed in the Department by individuals and by foreign governments.

    d. To avoid giving needless offense to other nationalities or individuals.

    e. To eliminate personal opinions presented in dispatches and not acted upon by the Department. To this consideration there is one qualification—in connection with major decisions it is desirable, where possible, to show the alternatives presented to the Department before the decision was made.

Recent editions of the *FRUS* series consist of a representative selection of foreign policy documents, including papers on policy formulation as well as the final decisions and diplomatic correspondence. Each annual series appears in several red-bound volumes, each covering the documents relevant to a geographical area or major foreign policy event, such as a great-power conference. The documentary history, now costing $100,000 annually to publish, amounts to 287 volumes through 1945.

The time lag before publication was only one year until 1906; it grew to four by 1914 and to eight by 1921. Secretary Kellogg's 1925 directive called for the preparation of the *FRUS* volumes "as soon as practicable after the close of each year." Since then the compilation has fallen further and further behind schedule—it was fifteen years in 1941 and eighteen years in 1953 when the volumes for 1935 appeared. The Republican Congress in 1953, eager to expose the wartime and postwar policies of Roosevelt and Truman, appropriated money for accelerated publication of the *FRUS* series. Despite this show of congressional concern, publication has continued to lag; by 1962 *FRUS* was twenty years behind events.[4] In 1962, perhaps recognizing reality, Secretary of State Dean Rusk established a twenty-year rule for publication of the *FRUS* volumes.[5]

From the point of view of policy-makers, the postwar volumes of *FRUS* do not record the events of a bygone era. The major events of 1949, for example—the division of Germany, the creation of NATO, the end of the Arab-Israeli War, the triumph of the Chinese Communists—still influence policy today. Although most of the statesmen of the forties have passed from the scene, lesser figures of that period—say, a Dean Rusk or a Richard Nixon—have played prominent roles since.

So far, continuing budgetary and staff problems as well as the controversial and sensitive nature of the documents have defeated efforts to meet the twenty-year limit. The first volume for 1945 appeared in 1967, and the first 1946 volumes in 1969, three years behind schedule. Apparently America's hugely expanded involvement in international affairs since World War II has made the compilation of the *FRUS* volumes a formidable task.[6]

The first obstacle to rapid publication is the sheer quantity of papers to be sifted before compilation and then chosen for publication. The *FRUS* collections covering the immediate prewar years averaged five volumes; in contrast the records for 1945

[4] Leopold, "The *Foreign Relations* Series," pp. 600–601, 605–609.

[5] Robert B. Stewart, "Report of the Eleventh Annual Meeting of the Advisory Committee on 'Foreign Relations of the United States,' " *The American Journal of International Law* (July 1968), pp. 725–26.

[6] The discussion of the postwar *FRUS* publication problems draws on the following sources: Franklin, "The Future of the 'Foreign Relations' Series," pp. 249–51; Letters from Dr. William Franklin, director of the State Department Historical Office, February 9, 1971, and May 4, 1971; Interview with Dr. Franklin in the State Department, March 30, 1971.

filled twelve volumes. In order to maintain a reasonable pace of publication, the Historical Office now limits its compilation to the most important records, covering less significant items in editorial notes. Nevertheless, the 1946 collection will fill eleven volumes when completed. Thinner paper, thicker volumes, and increased selectivity have resulted in plans for an eight-volume set for 1947 and seven volumes for 1948.

In the prewar years, the central files of the State Department contained virtually all the records of American foreign policy. Today, the State Department has lost its primacy to the White House and the Pentagon, and numerous other agencies contribute to foreign policy or manage programs abroad. As a result, the staff of the Historical Office, which is responsible for the compilation of *FRUS*, seeks pertinent documents all over Washington and in the presidential libraries.

Even the filing system of the State Department has become a problem for the compilers of *FRUS*. The production of records has exceeded the State Department's capacity to file and index them, and the staff of the Historical Office must search through unsystematic office and foreign service "lots" to find significant records, especially those related to policy formulation.

Even after the staff historians have succeeded in selecting and compiling the documents for a given year, they face a prolonged process of clearance for publication. The originating authority must approve the publication of classified documents in the *FRUS* volumes. To avoid seeking clearance from foreign governments, the Historical Office minimizes the number of foreign-originated documents included in its collection. But even in Washington, the clearance process can take as long as two years from the submission of galley proofs until final clearance.[7] The reluctance of the National Security Council to clear its papers for publication, for example, has held up the preparation of the volumes for 1947.

Officials responsible for clearance have had to consider the effect of publication on current policies and negotiations and the

[7] "Advisory Committee on 'Foreign Relations of the United States': Report of the Thirteenth Meeting—1969," *Political Science* (Winter 1970), p. 40.

possibility of embarrassment to individuals. The compilers of *FRUS* can usually delete compromising or embarrassing personal references without distorting the record, but unresolved policy issues pose a greater problem. If publication is judged detrimental to American policy, the Historical Office may have to omit certain documents, calling attention to the deletion in editorial notes and providing the file numbers of the documents for future reference.[8]

While some of the clearance problems can be attributed to political or security issues, much of the delay is due to the lack of priority accorded by the department to the publication of *FRUS*. Besieged by immediate problems, policy officers have had little time or interest for the examination of historical records. Often the most junior official in the originating office has been responsible for clearance, and he may be the most likely to err on the side of caution.[9]

The Historical Office has a lobby of sorts in the academic community. In 1957, the State Department established an academic advisory committee for the *FRUS* series, composed of three scholars from the American Historical Association and two each from the American Political Science Association and the American Society of International Law. Each year, the advisory committee has pleaded for additional personnel for the Historical Office. Finally, in 1970, the department requested two additional positions for the office. The advisory committee also supports the Historical Office in its annual battle for clearance. For example, the 1970 meeting proposed a policy of automatic clearance if the originating offices take no action within six months of the submission of galley proofs. The scholars also recommended that a senior Foreign Service officer be assigned to the Historical Office to handle the clearance problem.[10]

The *FRUS* advisory committees have also advocated earlier publication of *FRUS* on political grounds:

[8] For an example of such treatment, see Franklin's discussion of a U.S.–Mexican boundary dispute in "The Future of the 'Foreign Relations' Series," p. 251.

[9] Stewart, "Report of the Eleventh Annual Meeting," pp. 726–27.

[10] "Report of the Advisory Committee on 'Foreign Relations of the United States,' held at the Department of State, November 11, 1970," mimeographed, p. 1.

The Committee believes that in many instances the national interest would be well served by publishing the record long before the 20-year lapse. Here the Advisory Committee would emphasize especially the relevance of the historical record to current policy problems. In some cases American foreign policy would not be embarrassed—it would be positively assisted—by publication of the record. Having regard to the problem of both domestic and world opinion, and particularly as it may be affected by the current "outbursts of revisionism" by certain historians on the origins and nature of the Cold War, the Advisory Committee believes that full public documentation on the years 1945–1947 and even later, would serve highly practical national purposes. The ready availability of the full record on the origins and early years of the Cold War would help provide a sound factual basis for judgment and decision by our policymakers, by Congress, by scholars and writers and by public opinion at home and abroad.[11]

To date, the scholars have failed to overcome bureaucratic caution and inertia or the administrative difficulties of publishing the *FRUS* series. As a result, the no-access period has grown longer and longer.

Access to State Department Archives

Until the publication of the *FRUS* series, the files of the State Department are limited to official use. It has been noted by William D. Blair, Jr., deputy assistant secretary of state for public affairs, that the series is "the point of the declassification spear for the most important foreign policy documents, which tend to be exempted from the normal operation of automatic declassification."[12] Therefore, access to historical State Department records will be governed by its publication rather than by the provisions of Nixon's new executive order. In the past, the department occasionally published "white papers," including the official records of a controversial policy (for example, the 1949 China White Paper), but such publications occurred only in exceptional cir-

[11] Stewart, "Report of the Eleventh Annual Meeting," p. 726.
[12] Statement by William D. Blair, Jr., before the Special Subcommittee on Intelligence of the House Armed Services Committee, March 10, 1972, mimeographed.

cumstances. Until 1969, the department published an annual one-volume collection of official papers entitled *American Foreign Policy Current Documents,* which regularly appeared two years after the events covered. But staff shortages in the Historical Office forced suspension of the *Current Documents* publication.[13]

The private citizen can obtain official State Department records before the publication of *FRUS* through the similar procedures of the FOI Act and the Nixon executive order. Under the act, any citizen may apply to the Chief of the Records Division of the State Department for copies of specific records, identifiable by date, format, and subject matter. However, the department can, at its discretion, reject any request falling under one of the nine exemptions of the FOI Act.[14] The act is thus of little use for research purposes because scholars usually want access to the files rather than copies of individual records, and the courts are reluctant to overturn departmental decisions. Similarly, the Nixon order provides for departmental committees to review the classification of a document on request after ten years from issuance.

Only in very special cases can outsiders gain access to the files sooner than twenty-six years. While ordinary private researchers cannot use the State Department files during the closed period, the department and the Nixon executive order extend a privilege to former senior officials, who are given access to the records of their own official activities for the purpose of writing memoirs or for explaining or defending their own actions while in office. The department established this "old boy rule" to encourage former officials to leave their papers with the department in order to preserve the official historical record.[15]

The late Dean Acheson, Secretary of State in the Truman Administration, used the State Department closed files in writing his memoirs, *Present at the Creation: My Years in the State De-*

[13] "Advisory Committee on 'Foreign Relations of the United States': Report of the Thirteenth Meeting—1969," p. 40.

[14] "Availability of Records of the Department of State," *Federal Register,* May 11, 1968, p. 7078.

[15] Letter from Franklin, February 9, 1971; "Availability of the Records of the Department of State," *Federal Register,* May 11, 1968, p. 7078.

partment. He justified this exceptional treatment in the following way:

> As for former officials as memoir writers, they have something special to offer, as many historians have told me. The why of many events, the decisive why, is apt to survive only in their memory. The use of documents to me was most important more as a corrective to memory than as a supplement. My memory, I find, is often very clear and at the same time mixed up, sometimes putting people at places and meetings at which they were not present or as taking positions taken by others. The memoranda taken at the time straightens out a sometimes involved sequence. Furthermore, an active imagination or twice-told tale often creates the equivalent of Sam Morison's "Flyaway Islands," which bedeviled the early cartographers. If it isn't in the record, the memoir-writer should doubt it.[16]

The incumbent Secretary of State has the authority to limit the "old boy rule" when it might endanger the national interest. The department, moreover, can require official review of notes before publication of a manuscript based on classified information. Nevertheless, citations from still-classified records continue to appear in memoirs. As a rule, the department does not declassify records that appear in published memoirs, but the non-official scholar may be able to acquire copies of records used in this way. For example, Dr. William Franklin cited the case of the scholar who complained bitterly about Robert F. Kennedy's use in his book *Thirteen Days* of the "first" Khrushchev message of October 26, 1962, to President Kennedy during the Cuban missile crisis; because Kennedy had quoted from the letter and summarized its contents, the department could declassify it for the aggrieved scholar when he requested it through proper channels.[17]

Despite its obvious benefit for public enlightenment, the "old boy rule" does give an advantage to the participant whose personal account becomes a part of the historical record before

---

[16] Letter dated September 1, 1971.

[17] Interview with Dr. Franklin, March 30, 1971; Robert F. Kennedy, *Thirteen Days: A Memoir of the Cuban Missile Crisis* (New York, W. W. Norton & Company, 1969), pp. 86–87.

the more detached observer can arrive at an independent interpretation based on primary sources.

A second exception to the closed period is the special access occasionally granted to selected scholars to write authoritative histories based on State Department records. The decision to grant such special access comes from senior officials who are anxious to enlighten the American people on controversial events or policies. Works produced in this way include the studies of pre-World War II foreign policy by William L. Langer and A. Everett Gleason, *The Challenge to Isolation* (1952) and *The Undeclared War* (1953). According to Langer, these books could not have been written so soon after the event without access to government records. Despite official access, these were works of independent scholarship: The only reported official control was the submission of the manuscript for a security check by the State Department. Langer claims that all classified records cited in his books were declassified in connection with publication; however, other scholars have complained of being denied access to records at Hyde Park used by Langer and Gleason.[18]

In recent years, the Historical Office has forsworn the practice of granting special access to the closed period files. Dr. Franklin asserts, "For more than ten years we have not been accepting any applications for access to closed-period files, and there have been no special grants of access bestowed by this office on any favored historians. We have not been able to open the files as fast as I had hoped, but we have not taken refuge in inequity."[19] Privileged access for the purpose of officially authorized histories should be distinguished from unofficial access granted selected scholars for research on a not-for-attribution basis. Such "leaks" are beyond the reach of the Historical Office regulations.

With these exceptions, scholars must await the publication of *FRUS* before gaining access to State Department files. Dr.

---

[18] "The Historian's Right to See," letter from William L. Langer, *The New York Times Book Review*, December 14, 1970, p. 18; letter from Dr. William Franklin, May 4, 1971; *Final Report of the Joint AHA-OAH Ad Hoc Committee to Investigate the Charges Against the Franklin D. Roosevelt Library and Related Matters*, August 24, 1970, pp. 387, 396–97.

[19] Letter of May 4, 1971.

Franklin estimates that only ten percent of the annual accumulation of records is published in the *FRUS* volumes.[20] So during the restricted period scholars can get at the other 90 percent only under the security regulations first established by Executive Order 10816 and now written into the Nixon order.

Until January 1972, when the restricted period was eliminated for the 1942–45 FRUS records, the State Department provided limited access during that period to "qualified researchers demonstrating a scholarly or professional need for information." Researchers had to be American citizens, pass a security clearance, and submit their notes for departmental review. After receipt of written application forms, the director of the Historical Office determined the extent and nature of access privileges. The forms required information on the citizenship and academic credentials of the applicant, the nature and scope of the research project, the type of records needed, and the names of two references. Research had to be confined to a specific topic. The applicant signed a statement promising not to reveal any classified information acquired through his research except as permitted by State Department regulations. Possible sanctions for security violations included loss of access privileges and criminal penalties under the Espionage Act of 1947 and the Internal Security Act of 1950.[21]

The security investigation, which took several weeks, weeded out applicants with police records or past security violations. Dissenting political views did not disqualify potential researchers, according to Dr. Franklin, although an unauthorized trip, say to Cuba, might do so. The Historical Office rejected very few applications but, by the same token, comparatively few researchers applied, which suggests that the regulations might have dissuaded applications. About 120 scholars, including graduate students, use restricted files each year. When the research was completed, the scholar submitted his notes for review by the policy bureaus, a procedure that again might require several weeks.[22]

[20] *The New York Times,* July 11, 1971.
[21] "Availability of Records of the Department of State," *Federal Register,* May 11, 1968, p. 7078.
[22] Interview with Dr. Franklin, March 30, 1971.

With the *FRUS* volumes appearing nearly a quarter of a century after the events related, the need for an additional restricted period was not very clear. The January 1972 directive eliminated the restricted period and permitted the files to be opened immediately after the *FRUS* publication. Although this reform proved feasible for the World War II years it is not yet clear whether it will be extended for the postwar period. An alternative approach would permit restricted access before the publication of *FRUS*. If research in classified documents is permitted after the publication of *FRUS*, why not before? Franklin argues that publication of *FRUS* must precede access to the files because publication of the documentary history is the only organized method for declassifying such a large number of documents.

Before the issuance of Nixon's order, the State Department, alone among the foreign policy agencies of the government, automatically declassified its records after thirty years, waiving document-by-document clearance. The files were then transferred to the National Archives for public use. The handling of the 1942–45 *FRUS* documentary accumulation reduced the thirty-year limit to twenty-seven years.

Exceptions to the State Department's thirty-year rule include confidential financial and personnel papers as well as classified papers originated by other departments or foreign governments. Records in these categories are not opened to the public for fifty years and may be used by both official and nonofficial researchers only with the express permission of the State Department. Similarly, records involving passports and related citizenship matters, intelligence and counterintelligence documents, investigatory files and "other records the disclosure of which would constitute a clearly unwarranted invasion of privacy or a breach of confidence placed in the U.S. Government," remain closed for seventy-five years,[23] under present State Department rules.

[23] "The National Archives: Restrictions—Record Group No. 59, Rev. 8, September 28, 1970," mimeographed.

Department of Defense

Operating under the same general rules as the State Department, the Department of Defense presents the potential researcher with an even more formidable array of rules for access to official records. Each component of the Department of Defense has its own system of classification and access which will continue under the Nixon order. Although the programs of the Departments of the Army and Navy are quite similar, each has its own set of regulations and procedures. Certainly here standardization of procedures would seem appropriate.

After World War II, the Secretary of Defense established procedures for declassification of historically significant records of the military services, but the huge masses of sensitive papers and the lack of manpower for declassification frustrated this plan. At the level of military operations in each of the services, however, provisions have been made for nonofficial research in classified files. In addition, the various components of the Department of Defense have published official histories of military activities. Although these histories are written primarily for official use, some are unclassified and serve as valuable references. The department does not regularly publish recent documents, and publication of its histories does not result in the declassification of records on which they are based. The State Department, however, publishes some Defense Department records in the *Foreign Relations* series after the originating office grants clearance.

At the highest policy level, the Joint Chiefs of Staff do not permit nonofficial access to their files and have had no regular procedures for declassification, publication, or making their records publicly available. According to Colonel E. O. Post, special assistant for public affairs to the Joint Chiefs, the records of this division are "uniquely sensitive" because the Joint Chiefs "are by law the military advisers to the President, the National Security Council and the Secretary of Defense. Until they are declassified and placed in the National Archives, these records are available only to officials of the U.S. Government who must use them in the performance of official duties." The World War II records of the Joint Chiefs of Staff and the Combined Chiefs of Staff were transferred to the National Archives and "with some few exceptions related to intelligence matters" declassified and made public in December 1970.[24]

The military services at the operational level (planning and execution) permit research in classified records much as the State Department does during its restricted period. Restricted access in the Defense Department has begun as early as thirteen years after the documents originated but excluded records relating to foreign policy. Under the Nixon order the Department of Defense for the first time will have to observe a thirty-year limit on classification save for exceptional cases, and records classified beyond ten years will be subject to mandatory review upon request.

Shortly after World War II, the Secretary of Defense assigned to the Systems Branch of the Army Adjutant General's office the responsibility of declassifying noncurrent Army records considered to be historically significant and of public interest.[25] At that time, the Systems Branch employed as many as thirty full-time workers in the positive declassification program; now the equivalent of only one-to-two full-time employees work on declassification. The sole recent product of its program is the declassification of the records of MacArthur's Pacific command during World War II.

The same four-man office has declassified documents at the request of other government agencies—for example, records for publication in the State Department's *Foreign Relations* series—and for nongovernment researchers. As much as 75 percent of the requests have come from scholars seeking to avoid the inconvenience of security review of notes and manuscripts that direct access entails.

The Systems Branch also has handled nonofficial historical re-

[24] Letter of February 11, 1971; telephone conversation with Edwin A. Thompson, archivist in the Military Archives Division of the National Archives, February 2, 1972.
[25] Information on the Army's access and declassification programs is drawn from interviews with Cyrus Fraker and Paul Taborn of the Office Management Division, Systems Branch of the Administrative Services Directorate, Adjutant General's Office, September 2, 1971, and Army Memo 340-3 "Office Management Program for Unofficial Research in Classified Army Records" (July 29, 1971).

search in classified Army files. In the last four years, the Systems Branch has granted an average of fifty-one requests yearly for access to Army files. In 1971, 137 researchers had security clearance to use classified Army records. The program of research in classified records, according to the Army, represents a breakdown of the Army's declassification program. Because of staff and budget cuts, the Systems Branch has had to substitute restricted access for the declassification program.

Even under security restrictions, only a portion of the Army's files has been available for nonofficial research. Under the previous executive order, Army records were retired after twelve years and transferred to the Federal Records Center at Suitland, Maryland, or the National Archives. Some records dating from 1958 and earlier were available for nonofficial purposes, but Army records related to foreign policy matters dating as far back as 1945 remained off-limits. Because the Army has been so much involved in foreign policy since World War II scholars have had virtually no access to documents dated later than December 31, 1945, equivalent to the State Department's closed period. Presumably, under the Nixon order a larger number of documents will be declassified after ten years, but the most sensitive documents will remain classified and inaccessible at least until after the annual publication of *FRUS*.

Getting permission for access to the Army's classified records takes from sixty to ninety days. The applicant must complete a form detailing the subject, scope, and purpose of his research, identify the files to be used, and sign a statement agreeing to observe all regulations for safeguarding classified information. He must also furnish personal information for a security investigation. In July 1971, the Department of the Army dropped the requirement that the applicant disclose whether he belongs to any subversive organizations. The stipulation that he be fingerprinted was also eliminated in all but exceptional cases. The personal investigation is usually conducted by the U.S. Army Intelligence Command, Fort Holabird, Maryland.

Once cleared for access, the researcher finds himself limited to using classified files for background purposes only. Note-taking is permitted only "when the researcher can restrict the documents to only a few which are vital to his research project."[26] Notes must follow a prescribed format for the purposes of security review. Officials in the Adjutant General's office have the authority to review and release notes taken from classified files predating 1958 without referral to the Army office concerned with the subject, except in cases of special sensitivity. Until clearance, notes are considered classified information and cannot be removed from official premises by the researcher. Clearance of notes requires about fifteen days if notes are limited to fifty pages and if the material can be cleared by the Adjutant General's staff. Manuscripts based on classified research must be cleared for security purposes by the Office of Freedom of Information in the Army Office of Public Information.

Cyrus Fraker, a member of the Adjutant General's staff, explained that under the present system his office spends its time reviewing notes rather than declassifying documents. Under this procedure, every time researchers take notes from classified files, his office must clear the information for release, even if the office has cleared notes previously taken from the same documents. A simpler and more logical system, it can be argued, is to eliminate classified access by declassifying the documents themselves.

The Naval History Division is part of the Office of the Chief of Naval Operations. Its operational archives, established during World War II for official use but open to the public when security restrictions permit, is staffed by ten professionals whose responsibilities include the writing of naval history as well as research assistance and archival maintenance.[27] The archives hold some 10,000 feet of records, most of which date from 1940 to the present. These comprise the historically significant documents

---

[26] Army Memo 340-3.

[27] Information on the Navy history program is drawn primarily from the following sources: letter from Vice Admiral Edwin B. Hooper, director of Naval History, February 22, 1971; interview with Admiral Hooper and Dr. Dean Allard, director of the operational archives, March 30, 1971; and U.S. Naval History Division, "U.S. Naval History Sources in the Washington Area and Suggested Research Subjects," third edition, 1970.

on naval operations and the records of the Office of the Chief of Naval Operations and other operational headquarters. The archives also contain such material as sets of German and Japanese naval records, the personal papers of some recent naval personalities (for example, Fleet Admiral William F. Halsey), and the data relating to the disappearance of Amelia Earhart.

For access to unclassified material, the researcher need only provide information on his sponsoring institution and on the purpose and subject of his study. However, most—probably 95 percent—of the material in the operational archives is security-classified. When possible, individual documents are declassified upon request, but in many cases it is not feasible to declassify the large number of papers necessary for research projects. Items of information in individual records often prevent their declassification. In such cases, the Navy, like the Army, has a program of security-restricted access formerly under the provisions of Executive Order 10816 and now under Nixon's executive order.

As of 1971, the most recent classified papers in the archives, those originated since December 31, 1958, were closed to nonofficial use. Older records were divided into two groups. Classified records originated in the Defense Department before January 1, 1946, were opened to authorized researchers with the exception of groups of records specifically closed by order of the originating office or covered by the exemptions of the FOI Act. Twenty-year-old records were usually transferred to the National Archives, although some of these remained classified, and access to them depended on approval from the appropriate office in the Navy Department.

Access to records dating from 1946 to 1958, which were made available for nonofficial research in January 1971, was more limited. The Navy did not permit access to records originating in other departments or foreign governments. It also protected information on nuclear warfare, strategy, and technology, as well as information regarding intelligence, counterintelligence, communications, and cryptology. More important to the historian or political scientist is the ban on access to "information concerning the formulation of foreign policy, including related national defense policies, if originated by echelons equal to or higher than a fleet commander-in-chief, theater headquarters, military government headquarters, or a military mission."[28]

Within this limited framework, the researcher must submit an application and undergo a security clearance similar to what the Army requires. According to officials of the Naval History Division, these procedures take approximately three weeks. If an individual has previously received clearance from another division of the Department of Defense, he can use the same application forms for the Navy.

Like their counterparts in the Army, the personnel of the Navy History Division have wider latitude in declassification than the historical staff of the State Department. Archivists or other members of the staff review notes and manuscripts rather than submit them to the originating bureaus. The director of naval history, according to Vice Admiral Edwin B. Hooper, who currently holds that position, "has certain authority to downgrade or declassify all noncurrent naval records in his custody and all other naval records submitted to him for review, except for some categories where other concurrence is required." Hooper added: "I try to approach such actions from the viewpoint of service to history and historians, as well as the national interests."[29]

The director needs concurring authority before declassifying records concerning cryptography, intelligence and counterintelligence, unconventional warfare, superseded war plans, "the concept of which might still be applicable in whole or in part," research and development data more recent than January 1946, and restricted data under the Atomic Energy Act. Finally, concurrence is required for declassification of records related to international affairs "which, if released, might prejudice U.S. international relations."

Admiral Hooper feels that the Navy's experience with classified access has been "relatively favorable." Limited personnel

[28] Letter from Admiral Hooper, February 22, 1971.
[29] Letter of February 22, 1971.

and page-by-page clearance hamper rapid declassification, but Hooper thinks that Navy procedures have "mitigated a number of the problems associated with delays in the declassification actions. . . . I believe there is considerable latitude in administering existing regulations."[30]

Military History Programs

The various military departments support active programs of contemporary historical research and writing, which, like their archival programs, are primarily for official use within the government. Some of these histories, for example those of the Joint Chiefs of Staff, are highly classified: Their only readers are officials with proper security clearances.[31]

The official military histories are interpretative narratives, written by professional historians in the employ or under contract to the military department and based on official documents, including classified records. Their publication does not lead to declassification of the documents.

The Army's Office of Military History, established in World War II and staffed by professional historians in uniform, produced the eighty-volume work *The United States Army in World War II*. These volumes have been praised for their "high level of scholarship. Based as they are on the original sources they form the foundation for any subsequent investigation of this subject. Because of the books' workmanlike quality, future historians will not have to undertake this level of investigation again."[32]

Today, the Office of Military History continues to produce both classified and unclassified official histories, written by staff historians and outside scholars. Recent works include studies of the Korean War, the Army's role in civil disturbances, and racial integration in the Army. Work is in progress on an account of the Army's role in Vietnam.

[30] *Ibid.*

[31] For a discussion of military history programs, see Walter Rundell, Jr., "Uncle Sam the Historian: Federal Historical Activities," *The Historian* (November 1970), pp. 1–20; Louis Morton, "The Historian and the Federal Government: A Proposal for a Government-Wide Historical Office," *Prologue* (Spring 1971), pp. 3–11.

[32] Rundell, "Uncle Sam the Historian," p. 5.

The Navy also sponsors official histories. Samuel Eliot Morison, an admiral in the Naval Reserve and a distinguished scholar, wrote a series called *The History of United States Naval Operations in World War II,* published between 1947 and 1962. Another nongovernment historian, James A. Field, wrote the *History of United States Naval Operations: Korea,* which was published in 1962, only ten years after the event. Morison and Field and other private historians working for the Navy are accorded full freedom in their research, according to Admiral Hooper. Although independent scholars, they are also given privileged access to classified documents as were Langer and Gleason by the State Department.[33]

The Naval History Division prepares classified histories of recent naval operations for official use within the Navy. The current project is an account of naval operations in Vietnam that might eventually be "sanitized" for publication. Meanwhile, Admiral Hooper and other members of his department are working on an unclassified history of naval operations in the Indochinese conflict. The first volume will cover the years 1950 to 1964 and should be publishable relatively soon. This history will be limited to operations rather than policy and will, of course, be the official version.

Official histories, such as those of the military departments, raise several questions in the minds of academic historians: Can impartial histories be written by men employed by the organization whose history they are writing? Are official historians given full freedom to use and interpret all the sources as they see fit? What is the scholarly value of histories based on classified documents inaccessible to other scholars? Does the taxpayer benefit from histories written for official use only? To weigh such questions, the various departments have appointed committees of academic historians to advise on their historical programs.[34]

---

[33] Interview with Admiral Hooper and Dr. Allard of the Naval History Division, March 30, 1971.

[34] Morton, "The Historian and the Federal Government," pp. 5, 10; Rundell, "Uncle Sam the Historian," pp. 2, 17–19.

The Atomic Energy Commission

Primarily because of the special sensitivity of information on atomic weapons, the security and history-writing programs of the Atomic Energy Commission differ somewhat from those of other departments. Most AEC records are classified like other kinds of national security information under Nixon's executive order and are treated in the same manner as the classified records of the Department of Defense. Ten to twenty percent of AEC records, however, fall into the category of "restricted data," subject to special security provisions under the Atomic Energy Act of 1954. "Restricted data," like all information covered by statute, are exempt from the declassification provisions of the executive order. The AEC publishes narrative histories of its activities based on classified information. These are a help to scholars as well as a source of information on AEC activities for the public.[35]

Compared to other government departments, the demand for classified data from the Atomic Energy Commission is minimal. According to Richard G. Hewlett, chief historian of the AEC, his agency receives only about fifteen serious research requests annually. Because the demand is so light, each request can be handled individually and informally.

Under the FOI Act, and the executive order, private citizens can request the declassification of AEC records designated as "defense information," constituting some eighty to ninety percent of the total. In some cases, the chief historian can delete a small amount of classified information and himself declassify a report. Hewlett does some declassification review on his own, but he and his staff of five generally have little time for this activity. A division of the Atomic Energy Commission regularly reviews materials for declassification, a process lasting as long as three or four months. The pressure for declassification must come from the outside, according to Hewlett. Only specific requests will overcome government inertia. He urges scholars to bring pressure to bear for more rapid declassification.

[35] Information in this section is based on an interview with Richard G. Hewlett, chief historian of the AEC, at the Twentieth Century Fund, February 23, 1971.

The Atomic Energy Commission's rules for nonofficial access to records classified under the executive order are similar to those of the Defense Department's. The process becomes more complicated where restricted data is concerned. The Atomic Energy Act of 1954 set up the designation "restricted data" for information dealing with the development, production and use of atomic weapons. Currently, restricted data include information on atomic weapons and on the isotope separation process for uranium-235. The AEC commissioners determine what data must be treated as restricted, giving no discretion to the staff. For a scholar to obtain access to such data, he must pass a full background investigation as part of his security clearance which may take sixty days. Even with this additional security clearance, a scholar must negotiate with the general manager of the AEC and the commissioners for access to restricted data. The commissioners can simply deny permission without appeal. The AEC assumes that technical information of this kind will always remain sensitive, so restricted data are never downgraded or declassified.

The existence of restricted data and the strict rules for access greatly complicate the use of other AEC information, since restricted data may appear in the same paper along with less sensitive information. Because the restricted data are not segregated, the scholar wishing access to general classified information may have to be cleared for restricted data as well.

In 1955–56, Lewis Strauss, then chairman of the AEC, conceived of an official history of AEC activities to inform the public of the Commission's contribution to the important policy decisions of the forties and fifties and to encourage other scholars to do more detailed studies of the subject. Two volumes have been published: *The New World* by Richard G. Hewlett and Oscar E. Anderson, Jr., covering the period 1939–1947, published in 1962; and *Atomic Shield* by Hewlett and Francis Duncan, covering the years 1947–1952, published in 1969. Hewlett hopes to publish a third volume in 1976, covering the years 1952–1961.

In preparing the AEC histories, Hewlett has had completely unrestricted access to the files of the AEC. The studies are extensively footnoted with both declassified and classified documents cited so that other scholars can use the citations to identify and request access to AEC documents. Although the commission's histories are not part of a documentary publication and declassification process like the State Department's *FRUS* volumes, three hundred documents were released following the publication of Volume I.

A committee of academic historians, recommended by Hewlett and appointed by the commissioners, supervises the writing of the AEC histories. At times, Hewlett has wanted to publish material that his committee considered too sensitive. But on one occasion Hewlett disagreed with a committee recommendation that certain restricted data be declassified and included in a history and the commissioners upheld him.

The AEC adheres to a fifteen-year wait before authorizing histories to be published for a given period. The fifteen-year interval is necessary, according to Hewlett, to protect personal reputations and to prevent officials from destroying their papers to avoid public scrutiny. Hewlett also argues that fifteen years are needed to gain historical perspective.

Central Intelligence Agency[36]

The Central Intelligence Agency has no nonofficial research program. The records of the CIA—and other intelligence agencies like the Defense Department's National Security Agency—are subject to the most stringent safeguards. They are designed to protect not only the information—which may quickly lose its sensitivity or even appear in the daily newspapers—but, more importantly, to safeguard intelligence sources and methods. Therefore, classified intelligence information is limited, even within the government, to those with an official need to know. Classification and declassification of such material is so sensitive that the CIA classification manuals are themselves classified.

These procedures do not, of course, prevent the circulation

---

[36] Information in this section is based on a letter from Joseph C. Goodwin assistant to the director of the CIA, February 11, 1971, and an interview at CIA headquarters, McLean, Virginia, April 1, 1971.

within the government of the substance of intelligence reports. Foreign policy and military agencies all receive CIA reports, and they may eventually publicize the information in one way or another.

Selected scholars are sometimes invited by the CIA to evaluate intelligence reports. They have security clearance and access to CIA reports for official, rather than scholarly, purposes. According to CIA officials, these scholars may use intelligence information in a "sanitized" form in their academic work.

The CIA has conformed to the FOI Act by publishing its procedures for public access to records in *The Federal Register*. Anyone may request identifiable CIA records by writing to the assistant to the director. If the record is subject to the exemptions of the FOI Act the request will be automatically rejected. But CIA officials admit that the chances of obtaining records on request are slight.[37] Moreover, the new executive order exempts information related to intelligence sources and methods and cryptography from the ten-year declassification schedule and permits special protective procedures for these same categories.

The CIA does make available to the academic community a variety of unclassified materials. These include translations of foreign broadcasts and publications and collections of foreign periodicals.

Despite the important contribution of intelligence operations to American foreign policy and defense and the significant role of the CIA in those operations, no official history of the CIA is planned. Whatever historical writing is done in the CIA is for official purposes and classified.

The National Archives

The National Archives is the final depository for official records of permanent historical value.[38] Papers and documents trans-

---

[37] Letter from Joseph Goodwin, February 11, 1971; *Federal Register* (July 21, 1967), p. 10759.

[38] Information on the National Archives is derived from letters from Herbert E. Angel, deputy archivist of the United States, February 10, 1971, April 5, 1971, and May 4, 1971; from an interview with Angel and Frank Evans at the National Archives, March 31, 1971; and from a draft summary statement of "general restrictions" for access to records in the National Archives and Records Service.

ferred there are subject to various restrictions imposed by the originating agency or individual donor. Generally, restricted material includes confidential, personal, business, or industrial information obtained by Federal agencies; medical records; intercepted private communications; investigatory files; all records emanating from the FBI; citizenship and naturalization papers; and Department of Defense records concerning the military service of members of the armed forces. Access to such records or others covered by the exemptions of the FOI Act and executive order must be approved by the originating agency.

Access to atomic energy data, classified material less than fifty years old, and all records of the Joint Chiefs of Staff has been granted only with the approval of the originating authority. For example, the researcher wanting to use classified records from the Navy Department, housed in the National Archives, has had to go through the entire Navy clearance procedure and has had to observe the same regulations as those applied to classified files in the Navy's operational archives. In most cases, access to classified material in the National Archives is limited to citizens of the United States.

In 1970–71, the National Archives carried out a pilot project focused on the files of the Assistant Secretary of War for the years 1940 to 1947. The purpose was to determine the personnel and budgetary needs for a comprehensive program to declassify all documents dated prior to January 1, 1946, to be carried out by the National Archives. The project provided the basis for President Nixon's request for a $636,000 supplemental appropriation for the declassification of World War II records submitted to the Congress in October 1971. The House Appropriations Committee refused to allocate funds, but the General Services Administration budget for fiscal year 1972–73 includes a request for $1.2 million for a full year's work on the declassification program, which would involve documents stored in the National Archives, the federal records centers, and the presidential libraries.[39]

[39] Conversation with Edwin A. Thompson of the Military Archives Division, National Archives, February 2, 1972.

Under the Nixon executive order, the Archivist of the United States has been given permanent responsibility for systematic review and declassification after thirty years of all documents classified prior to June 1, 1972, except for those personally exempted by heads of departments. The new provisions for declassification after ten and thirty years will presumably reduce the number of classified records stored in the National Archives and the inconvenience involved in using them.

From the foregoing survey of how the executive departments and agencies implement the security classification system, it is apparent that classified records become entangled in a profusion of complicated and confusing procedures that frustrate and impede scholarly access and inhibit public evaluation of past policies and operations. All agencies involved in foreign and military affairs classify sensitive material under the broad authority of the President's executive order and exercise discretionary control over many other kinds of information under the FOI Act. Declassification at government initiative or in response to citizens' requests in the past only chipped away at the mountains of classified material stored in departmental files, federal records centers and the National Archives. The new executive order is intended to reduce this vast accumulation of aging classified records. But because of the various loopholes, the problem will not be eliminated; security-restricted research programs will continue to provide one of the few means of access to sensitive and important national security documents.

Chapter III
Presidential Papers and Libraries

The handling of presidential papers is a somewhat anomalous extension of executive privilege, for unlike the official papers of all other civil servants, up to and including cabinet members, the official and personal records of a President are not government property, despite the fact that they were generated while he held public office.

Since the time of George Washington, papers collected by the Chief Executive during his years in office have become his personal property when he leaves the White House. After Washington completed his second term, he sent his papers to Mount Vernon. His successor, John Adams, took his papers with him when his presidential term ended. By the time Jefferson left Washington for his home in Monticello, carrying with him the documents accumulated during his administration, the practice was firmly established.

From one point of view it might be held that it is only considerate of a President to clear out his desk and files for his successor; but from a governmental point of view, it is questionable whether the practice can be considered good housekeeping.

In the past, presidential papers have been stored in attic trunks, sold by relatives, and sometimes lost. Many of Andrew Jackson's papers were accidentally burned, and Millard Fillmore's son, on his deathbed, ordered his father's papers burned. Robert Todd Lincoln donated fifteen to twenty thousand papers belonging to his father to the Library of Congress in 1923 but stipulated that they remain sealed until twenty-one years after his own death. He imposed this condition "because the papers contain many references to immediate ancestors of persons now living which in my judgment should not be made public." The Lincoln collection was opened to the public in 1947. The collected papers of the Adams family were not opened to scholars until 1956 when they were transferred to the Massachusetts Historical Society. Eventually the papers of twenty-three Presidents—from Washington to Coolidge—found their way to the Library of Congress through purchase or gift. The papers of seven other Presidents before Franklin D. Roosevelt are stored in private collections, libraries and historical societies.[1]

The vagaries of the private control of presidential papers are illustrated by the handling of a set of 250 love letters written by Warren G. Harding to Mrs. Carrie Phillips, the wife of an Ohio department-store owner, between the years 1909 and 1920. The letters were discovered by Harding's biographer, Francis Russell, in 1963 in a shoebox in the possession of Mrs. Phillips' guardian, a lawyer in Marion, Ohio. Harding's heirs went to court in 1964 to prevent publication of the letters, and in December 1971 agreed to donate them to the Library of Congress on the condition that they remain sealed until the year 2014.[2]

The history of the disposition of presidential papers suggests how hazardous this exercise in "executive privilege" has been.

---

[1] Letter from Daniel J. Reed, United States Archivist for Presidential Libraries, August 19, 1971; *Final Report of the Joint AHA-OAH Ad Hoc Committee to Investigate the Charges Against the Franklin D. Roosevelt Library and Related Matters* (August 24, 1970), pp. 343–45; Bernard Weisberger, "The Paper Trust," *American Heritage* (April 1971), p. 41; *The New York Times*, July 26, 1947. For the history of the Adams Family papers, see *Diary and Autobiography of John Adams*, L. H. Butterfield, ed. (Cambridge, Harvard University Press, 1962), pp. xxiii-xxxvii.

[2] *The New York Times*, December, 30, 1971.

There was always the danger that valuable records might be lost to posterity and that subsequent administrations, friendly or otherwise, might be deprived of useful documents. Certainly, scholars could take no comfort from the prolonged sequestration of presidential papers, whether in an attic, a shoebox, or a library.

Since the administration of Franklin Roosevelt, however, the handling of presidential papers has been more nearly regularized with the establishment of presidential libraries that provide a safe and systematic depository for the records of the modern Presidency.

In December 1938, Roosevelt announced a plan to deed his papers, books, and correspondence to the United States. The library to house these documents was built with funds donated by Roosevelt on family land at Hyde Park, New York, and turned over to the government on July 4, 1940. The library was opened a year later, but it was not until passage of the Presidential Libraries Act of 1955 that the National Archives took control. The library is maintained by the federal government and is staffed by professional archivists.

Harry Truman and other postwar presidents followed Roosevelt's example. The Truman Library in Independence, Missouri, opened its doors in 1959; the Eisenhower Library in Abilene, Kansas, opened in 1966; the Johnson Library in Austin, Texas, in the spring of 1971. The Kennedy papers are still housed in the Federal Records Center in Waltham, Massachusetts, awaiting the construction of the permanent library in Cambridge. Herbert Hoover's papers were transferred from Stanford University to a presidential library in West Branch, Iowa, in 1966.

The 1955 Presidential Libraries Act accepts the fact that presidential papers are not public property; yet, it establishes a public facility to preserve those papers with public funds. The library buildings are paid for with private funds and built on private land and then donated to the United States. The National Archives maintains and administers the presidential libraries and hires the archivists and support personnel from the civil service system to run the facilities. The archivists, however, have little discretion in determining access to the records under their supervision. The 1955 law provides that

> . . . papers, documents and other historical materials accepted and deposited . . . shall be held subject to such restrictions respecting their availability and use as may be specified in writing by the donors or depositors . . . and such restrictions shall be respected for so long a period as shall have been specified or until they are revoked or terminated by the donors or depositors or by persons legally qualified to act in their behalf with respect thereto.[3]

The withholding and releasing of documents in presidential libraries was not covered in Eisenhower's Executive Order 10501. Nixon's new regulation does bring the libraries under the mantle of the present classification system. However, in including protection and declassification of presidential papers, it simply formalizes regulations that were already in force and provided for under the 1955 law.

Presidential libraries house personal and official records of a President as well as papers of members of his administration and friends and family. Each donor has the right to restrict or bar access to his personal papers in any way he sees fit. A former President controls both his personal and his official papers written or collected during his administration.

The constitutional arguments for the President's control over his papers were presented at a House of Representatives hearing preceding the enactment of the Presidential Libraries Act in June 1955:

> The fundamental and governing considerations are simple ones. The immediate White House office is a constitutional office. Unlike other organizations in the executive office of the President, it is not established by statute. . . . The Constitution itself, of course, makes no mention of the disposition of the records accumulated in these constitutional offices. Every president since George Washington has considered that papers he accumulated in office were his personal property. Under our

---

[3] U.S., *Statutes at Large* 69, 84th Cong., 1st sess., 1955, pp 695–697.

constitutional system, it is logical that the separate and independent status of the office should extend and embrace the papers of the incumbent of the office.[4]

A more practical argument for presidential control of records was offered at the same hearing by David D. Lloyd, director of the Harry S. Truman Library, Inc. He contended that if presidential papers could be thrown open to public scrutiny soon after the end of an administration, there would not be much privacy while the President was in office; few persons would write to the President in confidence and few Presidents would put their private thoughts on paper. "As a consequence, the ability of the President to function as an independent officer of the government would be curtailed, if not crippled, and our constitutional framework would be damaged," Lloyd observed.[5]

Presidents and other donors can establish specific conditions for the use of their papers, including when and to whom they can be made available. Moreover, donors can reserve the right to approve applications for perusal of their papers, which means that they have the opportunity to write their own accounts of events based on their records before opening them to others. Former President Truman, out of office nearly twenty years, still retains some of his papers in his personal possession. He has prevented historians from studying documents that he himself used in writing his memoirs, which were published in 1959. Even the State Department has experienced difficulty in obtaining clearance for publication of certain of Truman's papers for its *FRUS* series.[6]

Donor-imposed restrictions create the possibility of unequal access to presidential library collections, that is of one researcher being favored over another. A committee of historians investigating the Roosevelt Library reported in 1970 that some scholars

[4] Statement of Dr. Wayne C. Grover, Archivist of the United States, U.S. Congress, House, Committee on Government Operations, *To Provide for the Acceptance and Maintenance of Presidential Libraries, and for Other Purposes: Hearing on H. J. Res 330, H. J. Res. 331, and H. J. Res. 332,* 84th Cong., 1st sess., 1955, p. 28.

[5] *Ibid.,* p. 51.

[6] Letter of Daniel J. Reed, August 19, 1971; *The New York Times,* June 13, 1970, pp. 1, 39; interview with Dr. William J. Franklin, director of State Department Historical Office, March 30, 1971.

question the practice of accepting donor-restricted documents. At the December 1971 meeting of the American Historical Association, H. G. Jones, director of the North Carolina Department of Archives and History, proposed that the official papers of a presidency be made public property like all other official papers. But those responsible for presidential libraries view donor restrictions as the price that must be paid for gaining access to and control of such papers.[7]

In addition to restrictions imposed by a President and other donors, access is governed by executive departmental rules under the Freedom of Information Act and by executive order. In the case of classified departmental papers, the researcher must apply to the appropriate department for security clearance and may have to submit his notes and manuscript to the department for review. Whether a former President can publish classified information from his papers is an unresolved question. Before his retirement, Lyndon B. Johnson reportedly asked Defense Department security specialists to review his files for early clearance. The Pentagon officials refused permission for declassification. Nevertheless, Johnson clearly ignored declassification rules by reading from what he claimed was a classified memorandum during an interview with Walter Cronkite, televised February 6, 1970.[8]

The millions of papers in presidential libraries record the routine and the trivial as well as the significant events of an administration. Yet in an age of jet travel and electronic communications, the most significant discussions may never be put down on paper at all. To supplement the documentary record, presidential libraries have established oral history programs. Those interviewed, however, may also exercise their donor rights and bar access to the transcripts of their interviews.

The administration of records and access rules varies from library to library. Significant numbers of presidential papers have been opened, on the average, six years after the close of an ad-

---

[7] *Final Report of the Joint AHA–OHA Committee*, p. 431; Letter from Daniel J. Reed; Weisberger, "The Paper Trust," pp. 41, 106.
[8] Letter from Daniel J. Reed; Weisberger, "The Paper Trust," p. 105; James McCartney, "What Should Be Secret?" *Columbia Journalism Review* (September–October 1971), p. 41; *The New York Times*, June 13, 1970.

ministration. Additional collections are opened as soon as donor-imposed restrictions allow.[9]

President Roosevelt expected most of his personal and official papers to be opened for research purposes after ten to fifteen years, although he indicated that some particularly sensitive records would have to remain off-limits for as long as fifty years. He appointed a committee of three—Samuel I. Rosenman and Harry Hopkins, personal advisers and members of his administrations, and Grace G. Tully, his personal secretary—to establish guidelines for access to records in the Roosevelt Library. In 1949, Judge Rosenman and Miss Tully (Hopkins died in 1946) established seven categories of restricted materials: investigative reports on individuals; applications and recommendations for positions; documents containing derogatory remarks concerning the character, loyalty, integrity, or ability of individuals; documents containing information concerning personal or family affairs of individuals; documents containing information of a type that could be used to harass living persons or the relatives of recently deceased persons; documents containing information the release of which would be prejudicial to the maintenance of friendly relations with foreign nations. In addition, they kept closed communications addressed to the President in confidence, the publication of which might result in discouraging confidential communications to Presidents in the future.[10]

By 1950, 85 percent of Roosevelt's papers had been opened for research. A systematic review of the remaining classified papers at Hyde Park was initiated in 1970, twenty-five years after Roosevelt's death. Between 1946 and 1970, approximately 3,200 researchers had made 15,000 visits to the Hyde Park library. In fiscal year 1969–70, some 1,000 such visits were made to both the Roosevelt and Truman Libraries.[11]

The papers of the Kennedy Administration are under the joint supervision of government archivists and a screening com-

---

[9] Letter from Daniel J. Reed, August 19, 1971.

[10] *Final Report of the Joint AHA–OAH Committee*, pp. 346–47.

[11] *Ibid.*, pp. 410, 412; Weisberger, "The Paper Trust," p. 107; phone conversation with William J. Stewart, archivist at the Roosevelt Library, January 24, 1972.

mittee headed by Burke Marshall, former Assistant Attorney General under Kennedy, on behalf of the Kennedy family. The collection consists of 15.2 million papers, of which nearly 42 percent have been opened to the public since November 1963. In July 1971, the Kennedy Library staff released 3.3 million pages of White House files for public use. These files included originals of presidential letters, routine correspondence, and drafts of important presidential statements, but the late President's personal papers as well as documents classified "secret" and "top secret" were excluded. Joseph Stewart, the acting director of the Kennedy Library, hopes to release some secret papers after clearance in 1972.[12]

Lyndon Johnson took 31 million papers from the White House, 5.5 million pages on microfilm, 500,000 photographs, 2,010,420 feet of film, and 3,025 sound recordings. The Johnson Library, built at a cost of $18 million, including the Johnson School for Public Affairs building, opened in the spring of 1971 in Austin, Texas. The first 250,000 pages of records, all but 5 percent of them related to the education programs of the Johnson Administration, were opened on January 25, 1972. Meanwhile, the first volume of the former President's memoirs, reportedly based heavily on classified documents, was published in the fall of 1971. President Johnson established criteria for barring access to sensitive papers that might be prejudicial to foreign policy or national security; material that could "injure, embarrass or harass" any person; and material involving Johnson's family, private affairs, and personal correspondence. According to library director Harry Middleton, papers in the Johnson Library from the Departments of State and Defense that are classified "top secret" may not be downgraded or declassified for decades. The library will have periodic reviews made by the State Department, the CIA, and the library staff to determine which papers can be made available to scholars.[13]

---

[12] *The New York Times,* August 2, 1971, pp. 1, 6; *The Times,* London, August 3, 1971.

[13] *The New York Times,* November 9, 1969, April 11, 1971; Weisberger, "The Paper Trust," p. 40.

Some scholars are unhappy with the presidential library system because it imposes lengthy embargoes on research while conferring special access privileges on former Presidents and members of their administrations. These grievances came to a head in the Roosevelt Library controversy.

In 1968, Professor Francis L. Loewenheim of Rice University charged that he had been the victim of unfair and discriminatory treatment because the Roosevelt Library staff had failed to show him or even inform him of the existence of six letters from American Ambassador to Germany William E. Dodd to President Roosevelt, which he needed for his edition of the Dodd-Roosevelt letters. Loewenheim accused the library of concealing the letters, which were subsequently used by library archivist Edgar B. Nixon in his compilation, *Franklin D. Roosevelt and Foreign Affairs, 1933–1937*, published by Harvard University Press in 1969. Loewenheim's charges were investigated by a joint committee of the American Historical Association and the Organization of American Historians. In its final report, dated August 1970, the committee rejected Loewenheim's charges. It found no deliberate and systematic withholding of documents at Hyde Park nor any negligence on the part of the staff.[14]

More significant than Loewenheim's particular grievance were the complaints elicited by him and the committee from other scholars. Some of these scholars felt they had been denied documents made available to other researchers. Other complaints included the complex and seemingly inconsistent filing system used in the White House and retained at the Roosevelt Library, the shortage or inadequacy of indexes or other file-searching aids, and the failure of the library staff to render expected services. Most criticisms were directed at the restrictions on research, the excessively lengthy embargoes on access, the reluctance of librarians to inform researchers about restricted papers and the reasons for the restrictions, and the failure of the staff to notify the academic community about the removal of restrictions and the availability of papers. As a result, several scholars expressed feelings of un-

[14] *Final Report of the Joint AHA–OAH Committee,* pp. 423–24.

easiness and uncertainty as to whether they were being shown the complete documentary record at Hyde Park.[15]

In its final report, the joint committee made specific recommendations for reforming procedures at presidential libraries. The committee urged that directors of all presidential libraries improve existing finding aids and accelerate indexing of projects now under way. In addition, the committee recommended that the directors of libraries publicize to the fullest extent the general and specific restrictions that prevent complete and impartial access to their holdings and to publicize what has become open and available for research to scholars. The committee also suggested that the Archivist of the United States continue his inquiry into the feasibility of establishing for each presidential library, where none now exists, an advisory board of scholars who specialize in the period of that President whose papers the library holds. This board, the committee suggested, would concern itself with all phases of the library's operations, but particularly with its publication program and its relations with the academic community. According to James B. Rhoads, Archivist of the United States, the National Archives is considering or has implemented each of these recommendations.[16]

The late Herbert Feis, former State Department official and diplomatic historian, charged the presidential library system with failing to alleviate the problems of writing contemporary history:

> . . . the presidential and other memorial libraries will later on be of service and value to those who write of the safely outdistanced past. But unless present and prospective rules and restrictions are relaxed, they will not aid those who want to study and write about the travelling recent past. Their chances of ascertaining what happened and of being able to appraise it will be as hobbled as they are now.
>
> The creation of these libraries was bathed in the light of promised revelation. They were not conceived merely as memorials and preservative depositories. They were hailed because of

---

[15] *Ibid.*, pp. 342–43, 356, 371–73, 397–402.

[16] "Reply by the National Archives and Records Service, General Services Administration, to the Final Report of the Joint AHA–OAH *Ad Hoc* Committee to Investigate the Charges Against the Franklin D. Roosevelt Library and Related Matters, August 24, 1970," November 19, 1970, mimeographed, pp. 3–4.

the belief that they would enable the American people to learn more—and more easily and quickly—about their past. But the light of revelation is now so filtered through curtains of reserve that the value of these institutions to the historian of the recent past is still to be proven.[17]

It is to be hoped that in time the procedures adopted by the National Archives will more fully enable the presidential libraries to inform the present about the past. But this will not happen unless Nixon's executive order succeeds in limiting secrecy and providing greater access, largely through implementation of the new regulation for declassification in the presidential library system.

[17] "The Shackled Historian," *Foreign Affairs* (January 1967), p. 339.

Chapter IV
Classified Research and Politics

Quite apart from its effect in hindering timely appraisal of official policy, security classification as it has operated in the executive departments and in the presidential library system is a major impediment to scholarly research in the field of foreign affairs. Scholarship must be free of political pressures in attempting to provide an independent interpretation of events based on all the available evidence. Scholars have a responsibility to cite their sources so that other scholars may verify—or criticize—these interpretations.

Because of this professional commitment, the scholar is at times anxious to hurdle over the classification barriers. This quest for material has different motives from those of a journalist. Scholarly investigations require access to the primary sources. But under existing rules and regulations, the scholar seeking to study the official record in order to write a fully documented and verifiable account of events, particularly in foreign affairs, has had to wait nearly a quarter of a century to work in the archives.

The regulations for access to classified records under Executive Orders 10501 and 10816 were complex, inconvenient, and far from uniformly administered. But the scholar's complaint was not only against the administration of these regulations and excessive classification; it was also against the practice of selective release of classified information. If the rules had been strictly applied, if information were classified only when essential for national security and released after security review and declassification on an equal basis to all, the controversy over access would not have attained its present form and intensity.

There is, of course, no lack of analysis of recent foreign policy. Journalistic and insiders' accounts abound, along with the commentaries of the new breed of participant-scholars, the experts who now so widely serve the government. But the immediacy and firsthand quality of these interpretations are often marred by their partial and sometimes partisan viewpoints. Officials tend to use the documentary record selectively to justify their own positions; some have been known to supply information or open classified files to favored journalists or professors. And former officials can present their own version of events by writing memoirs drawing on classified material.

Restricted access under Executive Order 10816 depended on official discretion. The evidence was, in effect, preselected by government and might not be made publicly available for independent verification. To a far greater extent, the reliance on official or participant accounts and on leaks of classified information enmeshes the scholar in politics. The publication of the Pentagon Papers, while proving how valuable the documentary record can be in confirming or denying conflicting interpretations of the recent past, called into question the motives and justification of the classification system and it had far-reaching political repercussions. Traditionally, historians avoided political involvement by confining their studies to the distant past. The analysis of current issues, it should be recognized, cannot be protected from political controversy. Although the Pentagon Papers affair is very much in the forefront of interest now, it is far from a "first." An incident in the not too distant past, the running dispute over the alleged American "loss" of China, also involved revelations from official records.

In June 1945, the Justice Department arrested six persons—government officials and members of the staff of *Amerasia* magazine—for violating the Espionage Act "through the theft of highly confidential documents."[1] Among the accused was John Stewart Service, one of a group of Foreign Service officers who had been purged by Ambassador Patrick Hurley from the United States Embassy in Chungking for arguing that American aid for the Nationalist Chinese should have been made conditional on Chiang Kai-shek's acceptance of reform and political cooperation with the Communists. Overcommitment to the Nationalists, they felt, might leave the United States on the losing side in a Chinese civil war, while American overtures to the Communists might result in detaching the latter from their Soviet mentors.

Amerasia was a small, left-wing periodical devoted to Far Eastern affairs. The publication of a slightly altered version of a classified Office of Strategic Services document in the February 1945 issue led to the discovery of the security leak. The FBI found 1,700 classified documents, mostly concerned with Far Eastern affairs, in the magazine's New York office. The documents, some bearing a "top secret" stamp, had originated in the OSS and the Departments of State, War, and Navy among others, and included a secret message from President Roosevelt to Chiang Kai-shek, reports on the private lives of Chiang and his wife, on American and Allied military forces in the Pacific theater, and on plans for postwar Japan. They also included reports by John Service and other Foreign Service officers from China.

The government was handicapped by the difficulties involved in proving espionage and the unacceptability of most of its evidence in court. As a result, two of the accused were tried for illegal possession of classified documents and received small fines; the rest were never indicted. Service admitted to passing classified

---

[1] David J. Dallin, *Soviet Espionage*, (New Haven, Yale University Press, 1955), pp. 445–48; Earl Latham, *The Communist Conspiracy in Washington: From the New Deal to McCarthy*, (Cambridge, Harvard University Press, 1966), pp. 203–16; *The New York Times Book Review*, September 19, 1971, pp. 2–3, 18–26.

data to the editor of *Amerasia,* but was exonerated and reinstated in his position in the State Department.

The *Amerasia* case was never really resolved. Some observers depicted the whole affair as a large but otherwise not unusual leakage of classified information to the press whereby the officials involved took advantage of a lax security system to pass on classified information to serve as background material for a magazine that shared their political outlook. Others, taking note of the size of the security leak, the known leftist sympathies of *Amerasia's* editors, and the failure to destroy the leaked records, concluded that the purpose must have been espionage.

Compared to the public furor surrounding the Pentagon Papers, the *Amerasia* case received comparatively little public attention. Unresolved as it was, it did not succeed in provoking serious debate over the nation's China policy. That policy did not attract heavy criticism until late in 1946, when General George C. Marshall's efforts to mediate the Chinese civil war, after temporary success, finally failed to prevent open conflict. The Truman Administration concluded that the Nationalist government could not be saved without full-scale American military intervention, a price that it felt the American people would be unwilling to pay to save China from the Communists. So the administration was ready to withdraw from China, although pressure from the Republican Congress resulted in at least limited aid to the Nationalist cause.

With Republicans victorious in the 1946 midterm elections and smelling victory in the 1948 presidential election, Congress began to challenge the executive for control of American foreign policy. China seemed an ideal issue because of sentimental ties to an ally in whose cause the United States had already invested much effort, equipment, and money. In 1947, when the Truman Administration began its campaign for aid to Greece and Turkey to counter Communism, the Republicans demanded large-scale aid to Chiang Kai-shek, who was resisting Communism on the other side of the globe. In response to congressional pressure, the administration sent General Albert C. Wedemeyer on a well-publicized fact-finding tour of China. On his return, the General's report, which recommended substantial American financial and military aid to the Nationalists and a United Nations trusteeship for Manchuria, was classified "top secret," and the State Department refused to release it to Congress or to the public. The report finally appeared in the 1949 China White Paper.

The White Paper itself was the Truman Administration's response to the criticism of its policies in the Far East. After Truman's surprise victory, the Administration stiffened its stand against any further aid to the rapidly disintegrating Nationalist forces, causing frustrated Republicans to turn their wrath against the State Department, accusing Secretary of State Dean Acheson of sabotaging the Nationalist cause, and calling for a congressional investigation of American policy in the Far East.

At this point, the Administration judged that the time had come to explain to the American people the causes of the impending Nationalist collapse and the reasons for its policy of withdrawal from the Chinese conflict. Officials in the State Department had first proposed the publication of a White Paper on U.S. policy in China in late 1948, but Secretary of State Marshall had rejected the idea for fear of hastening Chiang Kai-shek's downfall. By the spring of 1949, the Nationalist cause was doomed, and Dean Acheson, Marshall's successor, endorsed the preparation of a White Paper.[2]

The White Paper, officially entitled *United States Relations With China: With Special Reference to the Period 1944–1949*, consisted of a 412-page exposition of American policy in China since 1844 and a 642-page collection of official documents drawn from State Department files. The narrative section was based heavily on the documents, most of which had been highly classified before publication. Acheson admitted that the White Paper did not present a complete picture of American policy in China because research had been limited to State Department files: "All

---

[2] For the publication of the White Paper and the response to it, see U.S., Department of State, *The China White Paper: August 1949*, reissued with a new introduction by Lyman P. Van Slyke (Stanford, Calif., Stanford University Press, 1967); Dean Acheson, *Present at the Creation: My Years in the State Department* (New York, New American Library, 1970), pp. 397–98.

the department files bearing on our relations with China during the period in question were examined, and a fair and objective sampling was reproduced in the White Paper."[3] However, he did insist that it was impartial, saying in his letter of transmission: "No available item has been omitted because it contains statements critical of our policy or might be the basis of future criticism. The inherent strength of our system is the responsiveness of the Government to an informed and critical public opinion."[4] Nevertheless, the White Paper was regarded as a defense of the policies of the Democratic Administration.

The White Paper failed to convince the Administration's critics or large segments of the press. On the contrary it provided material for renewed attacks on administration policy. Leading conservative senators labeled the White Paper a "whitewash." *The New York Times* charged that "the inquest on China is not the work of a serene and detached coroner but of a vitally interested party to the catastrophe." Congressional opponents claimed that the documents substantiated their criticism of U.S. policy and accused the Administration of deleting documents damaging to its position. On the other hand, some State Department officials thought the White Paper an undignified defense of American policy and a breach of confidence involving some recent official correspondence. Scholars, however, have found the White Paper an important source of reference.[5]

Despite the publicity that accompanied its publication, the White Paper probably did little to affect the outcome of the China controversy. On the contrary, the China debate climaxed in the partisan atmosphere preceding the 1952 elections and in the wake of the Senate Internal Security Subcommittee hearings on the Institute for Pacific Relations. Presumably to provide nonpartisan confirmation of the Administration's position, the State Department, with the encouragement of Secretary Acheson, authorized the late Herbert Feis to use the closed files on China

[3] *Department of State Bulletin* (September 5, 1949), p. 350.
[4] U.S., Department of State, *The China White Paper: August 1949,* p. iii.
[5] For the response to the White Paper, see *Ibid.,* introduction and pp. 6–9; Tang Tsou, *America's Failure in China, 1941–50,* Vol. II (Chicago, University of Chicago Press, 1967), pp. 507–10.

policy to write his independent account of the policy, *The China Tangle: The American Effort in China from Pearl Harbor to the Marshall Mission.*[6] When the Feis book appeared in late 1953, reviewers offered no complaints about his privileged access to Department files and had nothing but praise for his work as a well-documented, objective contribution to the evaluation of American policy in China.[7] But this evidence of the benefits of impartial scholarly analysis of the official record did not persuade the State Department to open the files to other scholars.

Even after the Republican victory in 1952, GOP senators continued to harbor suspicions about the contents of the State Department files on China. In 1953, the Historical Office of the State Department was accused of hiding evidence that would contradict the White Paper as well as of postponing the publication of the papers of the wartime summit conferences in order to protect the Democratic administrations. In response to pressure from the Republican Congress, the Historical Office began to prepare a special series of *Foreign Relations of the United States* on relations with China between 1941 and 1949 and volumes on each of the wartime conferences.[8]

In December 1956, the State Department issued the first volume of the special *FRUS* series on China, covering the events of 1942. The volume attracted little attention in the United States, where the China controversy had subsided. But the Chinese Nationalists on Taiwan resented the revival of the fourteen-year-old criticisms of Chiang Kai-shek's regime. For this reason, Secretary of State John Foster Dulles indefinitely postponed the publication of the remaining fourteen volumes of the China series. In March 1963, the State Department without explanation released the 1943 *FRUS* volume on China still bearing its 1957 imprint.[9] With the publication of the 1944 set of *FRUS* in 1964,

[6] Feis, *The China Tangle* (Princeton, Princeton University Press, 1953).

[7] For sample reviews, see *The New York Times Book Review*, October 4, 1953, pp. 1, 34; *American Historical Review* (January 1954), pp. 379–80; *The Annals of the American Academy of Political and Social Science* (March 1954), pp. 214–15.

[8] Richard W. Leopold, "The *Foreign Relations* Series: A Centennial Estimate," *The Mississippi Valley Historical Review* (March 1963), p. 606.

[9] *Ibid.*, p. 608.

the China volumes were integrated into the regular *Foreign Relations* series.

Despite these unusually early publications, the entire documentary record of American policy in China is still not in the public domain. What has been published has been drawn primarily from State Department records. The unpublished records for the years 1942–1945 remained restricted until January 1972, while those from 1946 to 1949 are still barred to nonofficial researchers. As the United States prepares to renew relations with Peking, information about American policy toward China in the recent past is still not readily available for appraisal by independent scholars.

In 1970, the Senate Internal Affairs Subcommittee published a two-volume collection of the *Amerasia* papers, including some of the long-classified reports of John Service and other Foreign Service officers. In the collection, *The Amerasia Papers: A Clue to the Catastrophe of China,* its editor, Anthony Kubek, tried to revive the conspiracy theory of the Maoist victory in China. Harrison Salisbury reviewing the collection, shrugged off such speculation but praised the work as "a gold mine of practical, intelligent, revealing information, exactly what a policy-maker in Washington in 1944 or 1945 (or 1971) must have in order to make intelligent decisions."[10]

The long history of the dispute over China policy had thus come full circle. Events, as usual, have influenced judgments as relations with China embark on a new era. But controversy over Vietnam policy is currently as heated as the dispute over China once was.

The publication of the Pentagon Papers on Vietnam provoked a rash of criticism about the security-classification system. In issuing his new executive order, President Nixon acknowledged these criticisms of existing practices:

Unfortunately, the system of classification which has evolved in the United States has failed to meet the standards of an open democratic society, allowing too many papers to be clas-

[10] *The New York Times Book Review*, September 19, 1971, pp. 22, 24.

sified for too long a time. The controls which have been imposed on classification authority have proved unworkable, and classification has frequently served to conceal bureaucratic mistakes or to prevent embarrassment to officials and administrations.[11]

The dimensions of overclassification were indicated by the testimony of former officials before the House Subcommittee on Foreign Operations and Government Information in June 1971. Arthur J. Goldberg, United States Ambassador to the United Nations during the Johnson Administration, informed the committee that of the thousands of classified documents he had read or prepared some "75 percent . . . should never have been classified in the first place; another 15 percent quickly outlived the need for secrecy; and only about 10 percent genuinely required restricted access for any significant period of time."[12] William G. Florence, a recently retired Air Force security expert, estimated that the Department of Defense alone has at least twenty million classified documents on file, including published commercial information and even newspaper clippings. He concluded that "the disclosure of information in at least 99½ percent of those classified documents could not be prejudicial to the defense interests of the nation."[13]

Overclassification is in part a problem of definition. The standards for classification, established by Executive Order 10501, were themselves vague and subject to individual interpretation. The executive order concentrated on information related to national defense, but officials used its authority to protect a far broader range of subjects. Information about American defense or intelligence operations potentially useful to a foreign enemy— weapons technology, intelligence methods, military strategy, plans, and deployment—accounted for only one category of classified records.

A second major category subject to security protection en-

[11] Press Release, Office of the White House Press Secretary, March 8, 1972, p. 1.

[12] U.S. Congress, House, Committee on Government Operations, *U.S. Government Information Policies and Practices—The Pentagon Papers* (Part 1) 91st Cong., 2nd sess., 1971, p. 12.

[13] *Ibid.*, p. 97.

compassed the records of current diplomacy, safeguarded to facilitate communication with foreign powers and the give and take of successful negotiations. As former Secretary of State Dean Rusk emphasizes, diplomacy is not a democratic game:

> Public debate and public diplomacy just cannot resolve the many problems which arise in the normal course of international affairs. . . . Privately, ideas can be tried out tentatively, a greater degree of frankness can be used in assessing one's own or one's opponent's point of view, compromises and adjustments can be more readily achieved. Many an agreement has elements which are both agreeable and disagreeable to the peoples of the respective sides. When the whole package is viewed, both sides might find enough benefit in which to be able to proceed. If the negotiation were public, however, it would be very difficult to make adjustments which might inflame the public opinion of either side, one's allies or one's adversaries.[14]

Beyond the protection of current diplomacy, the State Department's lengthy embargoes on diplomatic records reflected official concern for future relations with other governments and awareness of the political and personal sensitivity of foreign statesmen. For similar reasons, the internal process of foreign policy formulation was also shielded from public scrutiny. Secrecy improves the policy-maker's chances of controlling events while preliminary disclosure of policy may sabotage its success. To encourage full and frank discussions of policy alternatives, internal policy papers were also kept secret for many years after the events they recorded. For officials to speak their minds freely and advocate unpopular points of view—so the argument goes—they must be protected from the public's tendency to punish the unorthodox and seek scapegoats for unsuccessful policies.

But these invocations of secrecy often serve political rather than security ends. While important interests are thus protected, other values—such as adhering to open diplomacy or the policy-maker's accountability to Congress and the electorate—may be compromised. Moreover, serious abuses—such as the use of clas-

[14] Letter dated August 24, 1971.

sification to deprive Congress and the public of information about the substance of policy and its implementation—have been amply documented in recent years. For example, a two-year investigation by the Senate Subcommittee on Security Agreements and Commitments Abroad revealed a half dozen or more secret agreements with various foreign powers. As a result, Senator Clifford P. Case, Republican of New Jersey, and former Representative F. Bradford Morse, Republican of Massachusetts, introduced legislation, passed unanimously by the Senate in February 1972, requiring that all executive agreements be submitted to the Congress for its information.[15]

The Nixon executive order has expanded the definition of security classification to include "information . . . which requires protection . . . in the interest of the national defense or foreign relations." But it neither acknowledges the protection of diplomatic negotiations and internal policy discussions nor explicitly excludes them from security classification. Nor does it address the issue of secret executive agreements.

But overclassification results not only from deliberate expansion of classification authority, but also from the nature of the classification machinery. The decision to classify documents under the former system rested on the discretion of thousands of individual officials. In the Department of Defense alone, there were 31,048 officials with the authority to classify documents, of whom 7,687 could apply a secret classification and 803 could wield a stamp marked top secret.[16] It is hardly surprising that over 30,000 officials, each classifying information on his own authority without supervision, could stretch the standards of classification. Low-echelon officials might prefer to err on the side of caution in classifying material which might be "prejudicial to the defense interests of the nation" or perhaps politically embarrassing to superiors. Secret labels were stamped on memos merely to differentiate them from the reams of papers circulating in the bu-

---

[15] U.S. Congress, Senate, Committee on Foreign Relations, *Security Agreements and Commitments Abroad*, 91st. Cong., 2nd sess., 1970, pp. 16–19; *The New York Times*, February 17, 1972, p. 1.

[16] *U.S. Government Information Policies and Practices—The Pentagon Papers* (Part 2), p. 599.

reaucracy and to attract attention to them as they moved up through channels. In other words, security-classification too often was not an exceptional safeguard, but inherent in bureaucratic routine.

The Nixon order expressly forbids the use of classification for such purposes and reduces the ranks of officials possessing classification authority. But classifiers will still number in the several thousands and will have to employ their individual judgment in determining which information "could reasonably be expected to cause damage to the national security."

In the last thirty years, hundreds of millions of classified papers were collected in departmental files. The page-by-page review required for declassification in most cases ranked low among the priorities of busy officials concerned with current and future problems and enjoying ready access to classified records when they needed them. Pressure for declassification came from peripheral executive offices—for example, from the State Department's Historical Office in preparation for the *FRUS* series publication— or from Congress, as in the case of the Senate Subcommittee on Security Agreements and Commitments Abroad. Requests from the public—journalist, scholar, or ordinary citizen—under the FOI Act occasionally led to declassification of individual documents, but did not begin to reduce the piles of aging documents in government files.

If the declassification procedures of the Nixon order prove successful, they will help prevent a similar accumulation in the future. But records classified prior to June 1, 1972, remain subject to former procedures or automatic declassification after thirty years, whichever occurs first.

The Traffic in Classified Documents

Despite the extent of classification and the lack of declassification, the public does receive a great deal of information about foreign policy through official channels. Without going through the formalities of declassification, officials selectively publicize formally classified material. Publication, however, is not the equivalent of declassification, and leaked information is not in the public domain, accessible to all on an equal basis.

Much of the news printed about the foreign and domestic activities of the federal government is based on leaks. In defending *The New York Times* decision to print the classified Pentagon history of Vietnam, Max Frankel, *The Times* Washington bureau chief, described the special relationship of the Washington press corps and their official sources:

> Without the use of "secrets" there could be no adequate diplomatic, military, and political reporting of the kind our people take for granted, whether abroad or in Washington, and there could be no mature system of communication between the Government and the people. . . . We have been taught, particularly in the past generation of spy scares and Cold War, to think of secrets as *secrets*—varying in their "sensitivity" but uniformly essential to the private conduct of diplomatic and military affairs and somehow detrimental to the national interest if prematurely disclosed. By the standards of official Washington—Government and press alike—this is an antiquated, quaint, and romantic view. For practically everything that our Government does, plans, thinks, hears, and contemplates in the realms of foreign policy is stamped and treated as secret— and then unraveled by that same Government, by the Congress, and by the press in one continuing round of professional and social contacts and cooperative and competitive exchanges of information.[17]

Officials may leak information to enhance their reputations, to explain policy decisions, to seek public support in intragovernmental disputes, to try out ideas without prematurely accepting credit or responsibility for them, or to sabotage policies to which they are opposed. The government on occasion uses the press to transmit diplomatic signals. The annual debate over the military budget is frequently the signal for advocates of different weapons systems and levels of expenditure to leak contradictory estimates of relative Soviet and American military preparedness. Conversations between Soviet and American leaders—Kennedy and Khrush-

[17] Max Frankel, "The 'State Secrets' Myth," *Columbia Journalism Review* (September–October 1971), p. 22.

chev, Johnson and Kosygin—have been leaked to reinforce the President's image as either cold warrior or peacemaker. Former President Johnson described his 1967 Glassboro conversation with Premier Kosygin to Max Frankel the day after the event. But the official records of the Glassboro meeting are no doubt still in classified files in Washington and Austin, Texas.[18]

Official leaks indirectly serve the public interest by providing inside information about the decision-making process and sometimes even invite the public to voice its opinion before policy is made. But leaks primarily serve the political or personal interests of officials who control what is leaked, when, and to whom.

Retrospective accounts of government policy, based on classified documents, raise similar problems. Public officials can use their access to classified documents to shape the historical assessment of their activities without exposing all the evidence.

The use of classified documents, of course, does not necessarily indicate a biased interpretation. The best of the official departmental histories meet high scholarly standards of research. Their careful citations guide nongovernment scholars in their quest for classified materials. In the case of the first Atomic Energy Commission history, publication led to the declassification of some of the records in the study. The same can be said of the authorized histories written by independent scholars, for example, the studies of Langer and Gleason, mentioned earlier, which led to the declassification of the materials they cited. Unofficial studies by academicians based on records obtained through Executive Order 10816 permitting restricted access to classified files also depend on government discretion and involve the use of records not in the public domain; presumably other scholars can obtain access to the documents on the same basis. Moreover, these kinds of studies do not usually appear until many years—even decades—after the events they record and so may not be politically sensitive.

This cannot be said for the works based on leaks of classified records. A scholar, eager to investigate a current controversial

[18] *Ibid.*, pp. 23–24; James McCartney, "What Should Be Secret?" *Columbia Journalism Review* (September–October 1971), pp. 41–42; *The Wall Street Journal*, June 25, 1971, p. 1.

issue, may accept the materials on the government's conditions and note in his study that the research is based on unidentified records not in the public domain. Access to the same material may be denied to other scholars. The government thus simultaneously violates its own security restrictions and plays favorites among private citizens, while the scholar, despite his good intentions, casts doubt on the validity of his work, since the scholarly reader has no check against the documentary evidence.

Government leakage of classified information on a discriminatory basis has been clearly documented in the case of the United States intervention in the Dominican revolt of 1965.

Most analyses of the intervention were based on direct or indirect access to classified material. Leaks of confidential messages from the American embassy in Santo Domingo to Washington figured prominently in one of the most important journalistic accounts of the intervention: Tad Szulc's *Dominican Diary, 1965.* Philip Geyelin, formerly the Washington correspondent for *The Wall Street Journal,* had access to some secret embassy cables. In 1966, the Center for Strategic Studies at Georgetown University published an "officially sanctioned" report, "Dominican Action," based on classified files. Abraham F. Lowenthal of the Ford Foundation also had access to State Department files for his study of the crisis, soon to be published by Harvard University Press.[19]

The two accounts of the Dominican crisis that stand out as cases in point are Theodore Draper's *The Dominican Revolt: A Case Study in American Policy,* published in 1968, and Jerome Slater's *Intervention and Negotiation: The United States and the Dominican Revolution,* published in 1970. Slater was granted access to classified State Department files; Draper was not. Both have publicized their scholarly disagreements and have discussed the issue of access to classified records. However, the importance of the Dominican case does not lie in their charges and counter-

---

[19] Our discussion is based on: Theodore Draper, "The Dominican Intervention Reconsidered," *Political Science Quarterly* (March 1971), pp. 1–36; letter from Jerome Slater, September 4, 1971; interview with Slater, Chicago, September 8, 1971; telephone conversation with Abraham Lowenthal, September 3, 1971; letter from Lowenthal, December 7, 1971.

charges but in the evidence they present of the government's violations of its own rules.

In researching his study, Slater claimed to have employed all available published sources, the complete collection of OAS and UN records, and eighty interviews with key Dominican, American and OAS officials on a not-for-attribution basis. Slater was also given access to many private papers, memoirs, and documents, including some belonging to important Dominican personalities, on a not-for-citation basis.[20]

In the spring of 1967, after completing all of his research and most of his first draft, Slater asked a State Department official with whom he was personally acquainted for a chance to see the State Department records of the Dominican crisis. After some time passed, Slater was informed that he could see the classified files, at the time only two years old and not generally accessible for non-official research. He did not make a formal application to the Historical Office, and neither his notes nor his manuscript were reviewed for breaches of security. The only restrictions imposed by the State Department were that Slater not quote directly from the files nor acknowledge his use of classified materials. According to Slater, the official record served mainly to confirm the conclusions he had reached on the basis of his earlier research.[21]

In the preface to his book, Slater addresses the problem of using nonpublic sources:

> I accepted access to all such materials only on the clear and explicit condition that I would be free to use them in whatever way I chose, submitting the manuscript for clearance or approval to no one. The sole condition I accepted . . . was that no direct citation be made of materials from nonpublic sources. Because of this restriction, the evidence for a number of statements in the book cannot be disclosed. However, no important assertions based on access to nonpublic material will be made unless in my judgment the source is unquestionably accurate and reliable.

[20] Jerome Slater, *Intervention and Negotiation: The United States and the Dominican Revolution* (New York, Harper & Row, 1970), pp. xvi-xvii, interview and letter.

[21] Interview with Slater, September 8, 1971.

It is evident that there are important problems inherent in this procedure. Much of the analysis cannot be verified by other scholars who will have not seen certain materials, although it should be added that the use of unattributed material from private interviews is a commonly-accepted practice that raises the same issue. There is also the danger that I may have become somehow biased, corrupted, or at least . . . "co-opted," thus making my judgments, particularly when they challenge some of the accepted wisdom about U.S. policy, suspect. Nonetheless, it remains my strong belief that the value of more-complete knowledge about a highly significant event in recent American history outweighs all such problems. . . . The sole criterion I have been guided by is that of strict adherence to the truth; no relevant data, no matter on whom it reflected favorably or unfavorably, has been omitted; and the analysis and conclusions of the book are mine and mine alone.[22]

Slater was not told why he was given privileged access to the State Department files. He assumes, however, that the senior levels of the department "genuinely believed that their policies and actions had been misunderstood and misrepresented, and fervently felt that if the whole truth were known, and honestly reported and evaluated, the public assessment of their policies would be very different. I think they came to believe that . . . I had no axe to grind and [was] simply interested in the truth. And the 'truth,' they believed, would exonerate them."[23]

In November 1970, after the publication of Slater's book, Draper sought access to those uncited documents to which Slater had referred in his preface. William Franklin of the State Department Historical Office, to whom Draper first applied, denied that his office had given any classified material to Slater and referred Draper to Charles A. Meyer, Assistant Secretary of State for Inter-American Affairs in the Nixon Administration. Meyer also denied having given Slater or anyone else access to documents on the Dominican crisis. He refused to take responsibility for any

---

[22] Slater, *Intervention and Negotiation,* pp. xvi–xvii.
[23] Letter from Slater, September 4, 1971.

80

such actions of his predecessors and set out a policy of strict adherence to regulations.[24]

Denied the privileges enjoyed by Slater and others, Draper wrote an article for *Political Science Quarterly* attacking the use of not-for-attribution sources and criticizing the government for refusing to make the full record available to the entire scholarly community.

The use of not-for-attribution sources, including personal interviews as well as classified records, creates a dilemma for the conscientious scholar. On the one hand, the use of such sources denies other scholars the opportunity to check the facts and the accuracy of the interpretation. On the other hand, to reject the use of materials on a not-for-attribution basis may do unnecessary damage to the completeness of the research. In order to study recent controversial events, scholars, like journalists, have come to rely on material that cannot be cited. In the case of government records, only less secrecy or much more rapid declassification would prevent this practice.

The Dominican case is significant for its illustration of government practices. State Department officials ignored the department's rules for access to its own records; they clearly played favorites; and they violated the regulations for use of security-classified records.

It is easy to understand why officials decided to circumvent the rules in the Dominican affair. Critics of the Administration's policy had attacked their judgment and integrity. Official explanations had fallen on deaf ears or had provided further ammunition for the critics. The Administration chose not to publish a white paper, setting forth the official position in a definitive fashion. One scholar who has investigated the Dominican crisis refers to "an apparent *quid pro quo* [which] has prevented the release of either the Administration's 'White Paper' supporting its stand or the Senate Foreign Relations Committee's hearings reported to contain information damaging to the Administration

[24] Draper correspondence with Franklin and Meyer, November 12, 19, 20, 30 and December 3, 22, 1970; January 26 and 29, 1971.

position. . . ."[25] The Administration thus avoided the kind of political furor that greeted the publication of the China White Paper in 1949 and protected the privacy and confidentiality of its files on its own terms.

Until the surprise publication of the Pentagon Papers altered the pattern, officials relied on similar techniques to inform the public about decision making in Vietnam. Memoirs and participant accounts published by former officeholders or executive branch aides soon after they have left government service are the most important sources. The impact on the public of such articles and books is far greater than any scholarly study. Best-sellerdom, book clubs, and media publicity tempt the insider who hurries to recount his experiences in the corridors of power. This situation provoked Feis to comment wryly:

> May I offer advice to the men among you who are planning to make their careers as historians about the most promising route to advancement? Do not spend pleasant summers in foreign countries on fellowships, or grim winters in cold boarding-houses studying foreign languages; do not squander your meager funds on books. Train to be President, or if that job eludes you, to be a presidential assistant. . . . Then, after you have served as President, and either have been worn out by it or worn it out, retire to a sanctuary which will be named after you, and there in splendor become a great historian, largely at public expense.[26]

The retired official can unquestionably provide a unique perspective on the workings of government. But there is the hazard that the former President, retired White House staffman, or bureaucrat may, consciously or unconsciously, selectively use the official record to influence public opinion and shape the historical assessment of his career to his advantage, knowing the records will not become available to independent scholars for many years.

In the case of major controversies, such as that over Vietnam policy, former officials compete to tell their own side of the story.

---

[25] Howard J. Wiarda, "The Dominican Revolution in Perspective: A Research Note," *Polity* (Fall 1968), p. 122.

[26] Herbert Feis, "The President's Making of History," *Atlantic Monthly* (September 1969), p. 65.

The public can at present choose from among four published versions—by Lyndon Johnson, his press secretary George Christian, Pentagon aide Townsend Hoopes, and former Secretary of Defense Clark Clifford—of the events leading up to the bombing halt of March 1968. But the official records, which could be used to judge the accuracy of the conflicting insider accounts, will remain locked up in classified files for twenty years.[27]

The Pentagon Papers, a useful check on official accounts, although the material it contains provides only a partial record of the decisions that shaped Vietnam policy, is a selective and sometimes second- or third-hand account. The White House files and those of the Secretary of State were not included. *The New York Times* version of the Pentagon study contained only 5 percent of the documents. Under the new procedures, as in the past, three decades will go by before the entire record of the Indochinese conflict is available for study by independent scholars. The early publication, sometimes within three to five years of the events they record, of participant or other privileged accounts contributed to the controversy over the system of prolonged classification and restrictions on nonofficial research. What is the justification for protecting "secrets" once they have been made

[27] Jack Anderson, in his Washington Merry-Go-Round column of November 30, 1971, asserted that portions of the Pentagon Papers secret documents were used by Lyndon Johnson in his memoir, *The Vantage Point*. Specifically, Anderson claimed that when Judge Gerhard Gesell, U.S. District Court of the District of Columbia, in the government's case against *The Washington Post*, asked the government *in camera* to identify those parts of the Pentagon Papers most likely to jeopardize national security, officials cited the account of "Operation Marigold," an unsuccessful 1966 peace initiative.

The New York Times version of the Pentagon Papers lacks the "diplomatic section" that reportedly covered the Marigold maneuver. However, an account (The New York Times, ed., *The Pentagon Papers as published by The New York Times*, New York, Bantam Books, 1971, pp. 523-24) was pieced together from other sources: a report by the Central Intelligence Agency asserted that bombing raids close to Hanoi December 2, 4, 13, and 14, 1966, were "to undercut what appeared to be a peace feeler from Hanoi." The Polish member of the International Control Commission for Vietnam tried to arrange U.S.–North Vietnamese talks in Warsaw, but when the attacks near Hanoi began, the study reported, the meetings were cancelled. In *Vantage Point*, (New York, Holt, Rinehart, and Winston, 1971, pp. 251-52), Johnson discusses the Marigold affair, meetings between Ambassador Henry Cabot Lodge and the Polish diplomat Janusz Lewandowski, a proposed meeting with North Vietnam on December 6, the continuation of bombing near Hanoi on December 3, and the failure of the North Vietnamese to attend the talks on December 6. Johnson's account includes every item of the Pentagon Papers account except the CIA analysis of the bombing raids, which criticized their effectiveness.

public—possibly in a distorted form? What interests are served by such secrecy other than the protection of former officials from independent assessment of their actions?

It is too early to tell whether the Nixon security system will prevent similar practices in the future. The new order contains a strong warning against unauthorized disclosure of classified information, probably directed at anti-Administration leaks of the Jack Anderson variety. At the same time, the Nixon order provides for access to classified files by scholars and former officials without defining its procedures or limitations. The flaws of the former system will not be corrected without a reassessment of the problems of privileged access and the need for equal treatment for all who wish to study official records.

Chapter V
Changing the System

As the tempo of events has increased, so has the desire and need for entry into the archives of government by scholars. The Nixon order may bring about some improvement, but it is unlikely to divert scholars from their continuing campaign for early and equal access to the official records of recent foreign policy. The security classification system may finally be yielding to some reforms to eliminate the tendency of the bureaucracy to overclassify, to prolong the period of restriction, to place roadblocks in the way of access, to release data piecemeal and for partisan purposes—in short, to curb the abuses and to simplify the regulations with which this paper has been concerned.

But reform is not a simple matter. Executive secrecy and the classification system were developed in response to real problems of national security, effective foreign policy and rational decision making. Proposals for reform have to take into account these purposes so that the delicate balance between the need for secrecy and the need for disclosure in a democracy can achieve some measure of stability and credibility.

In recent years, scholars, eager to work on the problems of postwar foreign policy, have sought means of facilitating access to classified archives. The press has long been critical of security procedures, and Congress periodically challenges the executive's control of records. Members of all of these groups, addressing themselves to different aspects of the problem, have proposed three approaches to reform.

The first approach focuses specifically on the problems of the scholar in seeking access to classified records and does not challenge the classification system itself. For example, Ernest May, historian of American diplomacy at Harvard University, has recommended an enlarged program of official departmental histories, documentary and narrative, and of authoritative, chronological surveys of American foreign policy written by independent scholars under government contract. In addition to providing policy-makers and the public with a more thorough understanding of the recent past, May argued that these histories could also serve as guides to the official records for other scholars, and their compilation could facilitate declassification as the *FRUS* series does in the State Department.[1]

Professor Louis Morton of Dartmouth, writing in 1971, proposed the creation of a central historical office in the Executive Office of the President or the Office of Management and Budget to coordinate the diverse historical activities of the federal government, to promote high scholarly standards in the preparation of official histories, and to serve as liaison between historians and government.[2] An historical office might be attached to the interagency classification committee established by the Nixon executive order.

A major concern of a coordinating office should be a review of procedures for restricted access under section 12 of the Nixon order, formerly Executive Order 10816. Standardization and simplification of the rules would help, although there is always the risk that the least liberal regulations would be chosen as the model. The existence of clear, uniform rules, defining the avail-

---

[1] Ernest R. May, "A Case for 'Court Historians'," *Perspectives in American History 3* (1969), pp. 413–32.
[2] Louis Morton, "The Historian and the Federal Government: A Proposal for a Government-Wide Historical Office," *Prologue: The Journal of the National Archives* (Spring 1971), pp. 3–11.

ability of classified documents and limitations on their use, would give the scholar some notion of the treatment to expect in work on official archives and some recourse in the event of dissatisfaction.

Neither of these proposals nor the new executive order speak directly to the tendency of both scholars and officials to try to circumvent the rules by unauthorized use of classified documents. Accelerated declassification should reduce the temptation for officials to offer irregular access and for scholars to take advantage of it. But so long as records of controversial events remain secret for ten years or more, leaks are likely to occur. Scholars might hesitate to accept classified data on a privileged, not-for-citation basis, a practice that serves official rather than scholarly interests.[3] Those offered access to classified files could follow the precedent established by Langer and Gleason and insist on the declassification of any records used in research. The primacy of official and inside interpretations of history could be countered by a requirement that any publication of classified information would lead to the declassification of the records from which the information was drawn. The publication of official histories would be linked directly to clearance and declassification of the records. The former official, while still enjoying first use of his own records, could no longer monopolize them. Of course, under such a system, the release of classified records would still depend on official discretion. Officials could choose to remain silent rather than risk exposure of sensitive information.

The second approach to reform is automatic declassification, which minimizes official discretion. The age of the document becomes the sole determinant of declassification. After a certain number of years, all records produced in a given year would be

[3] From a somewhat different point of view, Professor Alexander DeConde, former president of the Society for Historians of American Foreign Relations, in his presidential address to that society, urged his fellow diplomatic historians to broaden their approach to the subject and rely less on official sources and consequently official favors. (Alexander DeConde, "What's Wrong with American Diplomatic History," *SHAFR Newsletter* [May 1970], pp. 6–9.) Similarly, Tom Wicker, columnist for *The New York Times*, in "The Greening of the Press," *Columbia Journalism Review* (May–June 1971), pp. 7–12, criticized the press for overreliance on official sources and the official version of the news.

declassified and made available in government archives. Across-the-board automatic declassification has been offered as the only practical means of achieving timely release of the vast accumulation of classified documents. Uniform rules for release of restricted information, if applied to presidential papers, would eliminate most of the complaints about the presidential library system as well.

Most discussion of automatic declassification has focused on determining the interval of time after which the risk of disclosure would be outweighed by the public interest in access to the official record. The present standard is the State Department's thirty-year rule, now extended by President Nixon to all executive agencies. However, even as cautious and careful a man as former Secretary of State Dean Rusk finds a twenty-year rule acceptable.[4] Ernest May, who also advocates a twenty-year rule, points to the dangers of partisan use of records and politicization of the bureaucracy if archives are declassified sooner. But the strongest argument for a twenty-year rule is the need to retain the cooperation of officialdom. Early declassification would be an empty reform if officials destroyed sensitive papers or refused to record their thoughts and opinions out of fear of premature disclosure.[5]

Nevertheless, there is pressure for shortening the time span. James MacGregor Burns, professor of political science at Williams College and biographer of Franklin D. Roosevelt, pushed the debate forward in *The New York Times Book Review*, by proposing an eight-year limit on classification:

> Given the "speeding up" of history, [the historian] should be writing and publishing within a decade of the event. A sensible time limit on access to documents would be eight years. This would guarantee a President and his agency heads and his envoys against publication of their confidential reports until after a President has left office. . . . Granted that no official should feel vulnerable because of fear that his reports would

[4] Letter dated August 24, 1971.
[5] Ernest May, "A Twenty-Year Rule," unpublished paper presented at the annual meeting of the American Historical Association, New York, December 30, 1971, mimeographed, pp. 5–6.

be quoted in histories (and hence in newspapers) within a month or two, is there any reason that that protection must be extended to 15 or 20 or 30 years? Even more, should we not impose on the official himself enough sense of his responsibility before the "bar of history" that he is willing for his advice and recommendations to be published after eight years' time? This is an equally good test for foreign officials communicating with our Government.[6]

Since the publication of Burns' article, a consensus has begun to emerge among scholars in favor of automatic declassification within ten years or less. William Langer cited his own experience in clearing his histories of pre-World War II diplomacy as evidence that declassification after five or ten years is both possible and not unduly risky for American foreign policy.[7] The membership of the American Historical Association at its annual business meeting, held in New York City, December 29, 1971, amended a proposal for a twenty-year rule to call for a ten-year limit on classification:

Whereas the general public and the scholarly world have a vital interest in the early declassification of federal records: and, whereas the present method of declassification is both cumbersome and expensive: therefore

Be it resolved that the AHA, in the interest of scholarship and an informed citizenry, petition the Congress of the United States for legislation providing: that all federal records be automatically declassified as soon as is consistent with the interests of national security, and in no instance more than ten years after their date of origin, except as hereinafter provided.

a) that the originating agencies specify at least one year before their records are to be declassified the specific documents, if any, that in their judgment should be excepted from this rule and the reasons why such exceptions appear to be justified

b) that the documents that originating agencies indicate should be excepted from declassification be reviewed by a committee, appointed by the President of the United States, con-

---

[6] "The Historian's Right to See," *The New York Times Book Review,* November 8, 1970, p. 43–44.
[7] Letter to the Editor, *The New York Times Book Review,* December 7, 1970, p. 18.

sisting of representatives from the National Archives, the relevant government agencies, and the general public

c) that the final authority regarding the declassification of documents deemed exceptional shall rest with the review committee.

Still, any proposal for automatic declassification, based solely on age rather than the nature of the documents, creates its own set of problems. Under a system which sets an arbitrary time standard for declassification, some records would remain closed too long while others would be released too soon. The AHA resolution meets the problem by its provisions for exceptional treatment of specific sensitive documents. But, unlike the present system, it requires the government to make the case for continued classification.

A third approach to reform involves the rationalization of the classification system itself, including stricter definitions and controls on classification, enforceable procedures for declassification related to the sensitivity as well as the age of the document and procedures for independent review of classification decisions. President Nixon made some progress in this direction with his new executive order by somewhat reducing the number of classifiers, tightening the requirements for classification, and providing sanctions for overclassification. His declassification procedures are also an improvement although they are faulty in leaving exemption decisions to those who have classified the records in the first place. Similarly, the authority to review classification decisions is granted exclusively to senior national security officials who have a vested interest in secrecy.

These weaknesses in the Nixon reforms are emphasized when compared to congressional proposals. Congressmen F. Edward Hebert of Louisiana and Leslie C. Arends of Illinois have introduced a bill, being considered by the House Armed Services Committee, to amend the National Security Act of 1947 by establishing a twelve-man Commission on Information Protection and the National Security. Its members—four members of Congress, four present or former officials from the executive branch, and four individuals appointed by the Chief Justice for their legal or judicial expertise—would be responsible for continuing study and review of all laws, regulations, executive orders, and classification procedures relating to national security information in the possession of the Department of Defense, the CIA, and the National Security Agency.[8]

More comprehensive reforms are embodied in another bill introduced by Senator Edmund S. Muskie of Maine in December 1971 to establish an independent board to supervise and review the security classification system. The bill, entitled "Truth in Government Act of 1971," calls for a permanent disclosure board to be set up, appointed by the President and responsible to the President and Congress. The seven members of the proposed Board would include two individuals with experience in the diplomatic service and either military or intelligence work, a representative of the news media, a former member of Congress, and a member of the bar. Their duties would include the definition of classification categories, establishment of criteria for declassification and for downgrading or upgrading classified data, and setting standards for access to official records.

The proposed disclosure board would provide for automatic declassification of specific categories of information, the duration of classification to be determined by the sensitivity of the information. The least-sensitive information could be declassified after two years; the most-sensitive information could remain classified no more than twelve years save for exceptional cases. The board would be empowered to consider complaints alleging improper classification submitted by congressmen, officials, or private citizens and to order an executive agency to modify its procedures to conform to the board's regulations. The board would also have the authority to extend the period of classification, at the request of a classifying official, a maximum of ten years beyond the twelve-year limit. The President would have the power to overrule the disclosure board within forty-five days of his receipt of its decisions.

Senator Muskie's proposed legislation also establishes proce-

[8] H.R. 9853, 92nd Congress, 1st Session.

dures for providing secret information to Congress and offers amendments to the FOI Act. In particular, it provides for *in camera* court review of secret documents to judge the reasonableness of a claimed exemption under the FOI Act.[9]

The timing and content of President Nixon's executive order suggest an attempt to forestall congressional action in order to preserve exclusive executive control of national security information. Even if his reforms match his intentions, the American public will continue to be dependent on executive discretion for information on foreign and military policy.[10]

Past experience raises doubts about the ability of the executive to restrain its natural tendency to protect its business from public scrutiny. Because recent leaks of highly classified information have at most caused temporary political embarrassment, the average citizen is justified in questioning the judgment of those who make classification decisions. Supreme Court Justice Potter Stewart in his opinion in the Pentagon Papers case criticized the classification system for violating the first principle of effective security, the avoidance of secrecy for its own sake:

> For when everything is classified, then nothing is classified, and the system becomes one to be disregarded by the cynical or the careless, and to be manipulated by those intent on self-protection or self-promotion. I should suppose in short, that the hallmark of a truly effective . . . security system would be the maximum possible disclosure, recognizing that secrecy can best be preserved only when credibility is truly maintained.[11]

Neither the executive branch nor the public at large can afford serious or prolonged credibility gaps if foreign policy is to

[9] S. 2965, 92nd Congress, 1st session, "A Bill to provide greater access to government information, and for other purposes"; Muskie press release, December 7, 1971.

[10] According to James Kronfeld, special counsel to the staff of the House Foreign Operations and Government Information Subcommittee, President Nixon, by issuing his executive order, deflected committee plans to consider legislation reforming the classification system despite the requests of the chairman, Congressman Moorhead, that presidential action be postponed until after Congress had an opportunity to act. The committee has included the new order in its hearings on government secrecy, but legislative action will be limited to restricting the exemptions to disclosure in the FOI Act.

[11] As reprinted in The New York Times, ed., *The Pentagon Papers as published by The New York Times* (New York, Bantam Books, Inc., 1971), p. 657.

be effective in its implementation and in attracting domestic support. The opening of government archives to scholars would help restore credibility by making possible independent appraisals of the past and possibly providing guidelines for future policy. But the problem goes beyond the needs of scholarship. The mechanical changes of the new executive order must not deter further efforts to prevent the government from protecting its operations behind a shield of secrecy. The coalition of scholars, the press, Congress, and the public has a responsibility to formulate a new approach striking a balance between essential security and excessive secrecy.

Appendices

Appendix 1

The Freedom of Information Act

Public Law 89–487

AN ACT

July 4, 1966
[S. 1160]
Public informa-
tion, availability.
5 USC 1002.

To amend section 3 of the Administrative Procedure Act, chapter 324, of the Act of June 11, 1946 (60 Stat. 238), to clarify and protect the right of the public to information, and for other purposes.

Be it enacted by the Senate and House of Representatives of the United States of America in Congress assembled, That section 3, chapter 324, of the Act of June 11, 1946 (60 Stat. 238), is amended to read as follows:

"Sec. 3. Every agency shall make available to the public the following information:

"(a) Publication in the Federal Register.—Every agency shall separately state and currently publish in the Federal Register for the guidance of the public (A) descriptions of its central and field organization and the established places at which, the officers from whom, and the methods whereby, the public may secure information, make submittals or requests, or obtain decisions; (B) statements of the general course and method by which its functions are channeled and determined, including the nature and requirements of all formal and informal procedures available; (C) rules of procedure, descriptions of forms available or the places at which forms may be obtained, and instructions as to the scope and contents of all papers, reports, or examinations; (D) substantive rules of general applicability adopted as authorized by law, and statements of general policy or interpretations of general applicability formulated and adopted by the agency; and (E) every amendment, revision, or repeal of the foregoing. Except to the extent that a person has actual and timely notice of the terms thereof, no person shall in any manner be required to resort to, or be adversely affected by any matter required to be published in the Federal Register and not so published. For purposes of this subsection, matter which is reasonably available to the class of persons affected thereby shall be deemed published in the Federal Register when incorporated by reference therein with the approval of the Director of the Federal Register.

"(b) AGENCY OPINIONS AND ORDERS.—Every agency shall, in accordance with published rules, make available for public inspection and copying (A) all final opinions (including concurring and dissenting opinions) and all orders made in the adjudication of cases, (B) those statements of policy and interpretations which have been adopted by the agency and are not published in the Federal Register, and (C) administrative staff manuals and instructions to staff that affect any member of the public, unless such materials are promptly published and copies offered for sale. To the extent required to prevent a clearly unwarranted invasion of personal privacy, an agency may delete identifying details when it makes available or publishes an opinion, statement of policy, interpretation, or staff manual or instruction: *Provided,* That in every case the justification for the deletion must be fully explained in writing. Every agency also shall maintain and make available for public inspection and copying a current index providing identifying information for the public as to any matter which is issued, adopted, or promulgated after the effective date of this Act and which is required by this subsection to be made available or published. No final order, opinion, statement of policy, interpretation, or staff manual or instruction that affects any member of the public may be relied upon, used or cited as precedent by an agency against any private party unless it has been indexed and either made available or published as provided by this subsection or unless that private party shall have actual and timely notice of the terms thereof.

"(c) AGENCY RECORDS.—Except with respect to the records made available pursuant to subsections (a) and (b), every agency shall, upon request for identifiable records made in accordance with published rules stating the time, place, fees to the extent authorized by statute and procedure to be followed, make such records promptly available to any person. Upon complaint, the district court of the United States in the district in which the complainant resides, or has his principal place of business, or in which the agency records are situated shall have jurisdiction to enjoin the agency from the withholding of agency records and to order the production of any agency records improperly withheld from the complainant. In such cases the court shall determine the matter de novo and the burden shall be upon the agency to sustain its action. In the event of noncompliance with the court's order, the district court may punish the responsible officers for contempt. Except as to those causes which the court deems of greater importance, proceedings before the district court as authorized by this subsection shall take precedence on the docket over all other causes and shall be assigned for hearing and trial at the earliest practicable date and expedited in every way.

"(d) AGENCY PROCEEDINGS.—Every agency having more than one member shall keep a record of the final votes of each member in every agency proceeding and such record shall be available for public inspection.

"(e) EXEMPTIONS.—The provisions of this section shall not be applicable to matters that are (1) specifically required by Executive order to be kept secret in the interest of the national defense or foreign policy; (2) related solely to the internal personnel rules and practices of any agency; (3) specifically exempted from disclosure by statute; (4) trade secrets and commercial or financial information obtained from any person and privileged or confidential; (5) inter-agency or intra-agency memorandums or letters which would not be available by law to a private party in litigation with the agency; (6) personnel and medical files and similar files the disclosure of which would constitute a clearly unwarranted invasion of personal privacy; (7) investigatory files compiled for law enforcement purposes except to the extent available by law to a private party; (8) contained in or related to examination, operating, or condition reports prepared by, on behalf of, or for the use of any agency responsible for the regulation or supervision of financial institutions; and (9) geological and geophysical information and data (including maps) concerning wells.

"(f) LIMITATION OF EXEMPTIONS.—Nothing in this section authorizes withholding of information or limiting the availability of records to the public except as specifically stated in this section, nor shall this section be authority to withhold information from Congress.

"(g) PRIVATE PARTY.—As used in this section, 'private party' means any party other than an agency.

"(h) EFFECTIVE DATE.—This amendment shall become effective one year following the date of the enactment of this Act."

Approved July 4, 1966.

Appendix 2

President Nixon's Executive Order on Security Classification

EXECUTIVE ORDER 11652
March 8, 1972

CLASSIFICATION AND DECLASSIFICATION OF NATIONAL
SECURITY INFORMATION AND MATERIAL

The interests of the United States and its citizens are best served by making information regarding the affairs of Government readily available to the public. This concept of an informed citizenry is reflected in the Freedom of Information Act and in the current public information policies of the executive branch.

Within the Federal Government there is some official information and material which, because it bears directly on the effectiveness of our national defense and the conduct of our foreign relations, must be subject to some constraints for the security of our Nation and the safety of our people and our allies. To protect against actions hostile to the United States, of both an overt and covert nature, it is essential that such official information and material be given only limited dissemination.

This official information or material, referred to as classified information or material in this order, is expressly exempted from public disclosure by Section 552(b)(1) of Title 5, United States Code. Wrongful disclosure of such information or material is recognized in the Federal Criminal Code as providing a basis for prosecution.

To ensure that such information and material is protected, but only to the extent and for such period as is necessary, this order identifies the information to be protected, prescribes classification, downgrading, declassification and safeguarding procedures to be followed, and establishes a monitoring system to ensure its effectiveness.

NOW, THEREFORE, by virtue of the authority vested in me by the Constitution and statutes of the United States, it is hereby ordered:

Section 1. Security Classification Categories. Official information or material which requires protection against unauthorized disclosure in the interest of the national defense or foreign relations of the United States (hereinafter collectively termed "national security") shall be classified in one of three categories, namely "Top Secret," "Secret," or "Confidential," depending upon the degree of its significance to national security. No other categories shall be used to identify official information or material as requiring protection in the interest of national security, except as otherwise expressly provided by statute. These classification categories are defined as follows:

(A) *"Top Secret."* "Top Secret" refers to that national security information or material which requires the highest degree of protection. The test for assigning "Top Secret" classification shall be whether its unauthorized disclosure could reasonably be expected to cause exceptionally grave damage to the national security. Examples of "exceptionally grave damage" include armed hostilities against the United States or its allies; disruption of foreign relations vitally affecting the national security; the compromise of vital national defense plans or complex cryptologic and communications intelligence systems; the revelation of sensitive intelligence operations; and the disclosure of scientific or technological developments vital to national security. This classification shall be used with the utmost restraint.

(B) *"Secret."* "Secret" refers to that national security information or material which requires a substantial degree of protection. The test for assigning "Secret" classification shall be whether its unauthorized disclosure could reasonably be expected to cause serious damage to the national security. Examples of "serious damage" include disruption of foreign relations significantly affecting the national security; significant impairment of a program or policy directly related to the national security; revelation of significant military plans or intelligence operations; and compromise of significant scientific or technological developments relating to national security. The classification "Secret" shall be sparingly used.

(C) *"Confidential."* "Confidential" refers to that national security information or material which requires protection. The test for assigning "Confidential" classification shall be whether its unauthorized disclosure could reasonably be expected to cause damage to the national security.

Section 2. Authority to Classify. The authority to originally classify information or material under this order shall be restricted solely to those offices within the executive branch which are concerned with matters of national security, and shall be limited to the minimum number absolutely required for efficient administration. Except as the context may otherwise indicate, the term "Department" as used in this order shall include agency or other governmental unit.

(A) The authority to originally classify information or material under this order as "Top Secret" shall be exercised only by such officials as the President may designate in writing and by:

(1) The heads of the Departments listed below;

(2) Such of their senior principal deputies and assistants as the heads of such Departments may designate in writing; and

(3) Such heads and senior principal deputies and assistants of major elements of such Departments, as the heads of such Departments may designate in writing.

Such offices in the Executive Office of the President as the President may designate in writing
Central Intelligence Agency
Atomic Energy Commission
Department of State
Department of the Treasury
Department of Defense
Department of the Army
Department of the Navy
Department of the Air Force
United States Arms Control and Disarmament Agency
Department of Justice
National Aeronautics and Space Administration
Agency for International Development

(B) The authority to originally classify information or material under this order as "Secret" shall be exercised only by:

(1) Officials who have "Top Secret" classification authority;

(2) Such subordinates as officials with "Top Secret" classification authority under (A) (1) and (2) above may designate in writing; and (3) The heads of the following named Departments and such senior principal deputies or assistants as they may designate in writing.

Department of Transportation
Federal Communications Commission
Export-Import Bank of the United States
Department of Commerce
United States Civil Service Commission
United States Information Agency
General Services Administration
Department of Health, Education, and Welfare
Civil Aeronautics Board
Federal Maritime Commission
Federal Power Commission
National Science Foundation
Overseas Private Investment Corporation

(C) The authority to originally classify information or material under this order as "Confidential" may be exercised by officials who have "Top Secret" or "Secret" classification authority and such officials as they may designate in writing.

(D) Any Department not referred to herein and any Department or unit established hereafter shall not have authority to originally classify information or material under this order, unless specifically authorized hereafter by an Executive order.

Section 3. Authority to Downgrade and Declassify. The authority to downgrade and declassify national security information or material shall be exercised as follows:

(A) Information or material may be downgraded or declassified by the official authorizing the original classification, by a successor in capacity or by a supervisory official of either.

(B) Downgrading and declassification authority may also be exercised by an official specifically authorized under regulations issued by the head of the Department listed in Sections 2(A) or (B) hereof.

(C) In the case of classified information or material officially transferred by or pursuant to statute or Executive order in conjunction with a transfer of function and not merely for storage purposes, the receiving Department shall be deemed to be the originating Department for all purposes under this order including downgrading and declassification.

(D) In the case of classified information or material not officially transferred within (C) above, but originated in a Department which has since ceased to exist, each Department in possession shall be deemed to be the originating Department for all purposes under this order. Such information or material may be downgraded and declassified by the Department in possession after consulting with any other Departments having an interest in the subject matter.

(E) Classified information or material transferred to the General Services Administration for accession into the Archives of the United States shall be downgraded and declassified by the Archivist of the United States in accordance with this order, directives of the President issued through the

National Security Council and pertinent regulations of the Departments. (F) Classified information or material with special markings, as described in Section 8, shall be downgraded and declassified as required by law and governing regulations.

Section 4. Classification. Each person possessing classifying authority shall be held accountable for the propriety of the classifications attributed to him. Both unnecessary classification and over-classification shall be avoided. Classification shall be solely on the basis of national security considerations. In no case shall information be classified in order to conceal inefficiency or administrative error, to prevent embarrassment to a person or Department, to restrain competition or independent initiative, or to prevent for any other reason the release of information which does not require protection in the interest of national security. The following rules shall apply to classification of information under this order:

(A) *Documents in General.* Each classified document shall show on its face its classification and whether it is subject to or exempt from the General Declassification Schedule. It shall also show the office of origin, the date of preparation and classification and, to the extent practicable, be so marked as to indicate which portions are classified, at what level, and which portions are not classified in order to facilitate excerpting and other use. Material containing references to classified materials, which references do not reveal classified information, shall not be classified.

(B) *Identification of Classifying Authority.* Unless the Department involved shall have provided some other method of identifying the individual at the highest level that authorized classification in each case, material classified under this order shall indicate on its face the identity of the highest authority authorizing the classification. Where the individual who signs or otherwise authenticates a document or item has also authorized the classification, no further annotation as to his identity is required.

(C) *Information or Material Furnished by a Foreign Government or International Organization.* Classified information or material furnished to the United States by a foreign government or international organization shall either retain its original classification or be assigned a United States classification. In either case, the classification shall assure a degree of protection equivalent to that required by the government or international organization which furnished the information or material.

(D) *Classification Responsibilities.* A holder of classified information or material shall observe and respect the classification assigned by the originator. If a holder believes that there is unnecessary classification, that the assigned classification is improper, or that the document is subject to declassification under this order, he shall so inform the originator who shall thereupon re-examine the classification.

Section 5. Declassification and Downgrading. Classified information and material, unless declassified earlier by the original classifying authority, shall be declassified and downgraded in accordance with the following rules:

(A) *General Declassification Schedule.*

(1) *"Top Secret."* Information or material originally classified "Top Secret" shall become automatically downgraded to "Secret" at the end of the second full calendar year following the year in which it was

originated, downgraded to "Confidential" at the end of the fourth full calendar year following the year in which it was originated, and declassified at the end of the tenth full calendar year following the year in which it was originated.

(2) "*Secret.*" Information and material originally classified "Secret" shall become automatically downgraded to "Confidential" at the end of the second full calendar year following the year in which it was originated, and declassified at the end of the eighth full calendar year following the year in which it was originated.

(3) "*Confidential.*" Information and material originally classified "Confidential" shall become automatically declassified at the end of the sixth full calendar year following the year in which it was originated.

(B) *Exemptions from General Declassification Schedule.* Certain classified information or material may warrant some degree of protection for a period exceeding that provided in the General Declassification Schedule. An official authorized to originally classify information or material "Top Secret" may exempt from the General Declassification Schedule any level of classified information or material originated by him or under his supervision if it falls within one of the categories described below. In each case such official shall specify in writing on the material the exemption category being claimed and, unless impossible, a date or event for automatic declassification. The use of the exemption authority shall be kept to the absolute minimum consistent with national security requirements and shall be restricted to the following categories:

(1) Classified information or material furnished by foreign governments or international organizations and held by the United States on the understanding that it be kept in confidence.

(2) Classified information or material specifically covered by statute, or pertaining to cryptography, or disclosing intelligence sources or methods.

(3) Classified information or material disclosing a system, plan, installation, project or specific foreign relations matter the continuing protection of which is essential to the national security.

(4) Classified information or material the disclosure of which would place a person in immediate jeopardy.

(C) *Mandatory Review of Exempted Material.* All classified information and material originated after the effective date of this order which is exempted under (B) above from the General Declassification Schedule shall be subject to a classification review by the originating Department at any time after the expiration of ten years from the date of origin provided:

(1) A Department or member of the public requests a review;

(2) The request describes the record with sufficient particularity to enable the Department to identify it; and

(3) The record can be obtained with only a reasonable amount of effort.

Information or material which no longer qualifies for exemption under (B) above shall be declassified. Information or material continuing to qualify under (B) shall be so marked and, unless impossible, a date for automatic declassification shall be set.

(D) *Applicability of the General Declassification Schedule to Previously Classified Material.* Information or material classified before the effective date of this order and which is assigned to Group 4 under Executive Order No. 10501, as amended by Executive Order No. 10964, shall be subject to the General Declassification Schedule. All other information or material classified before the effective date of this order, whether or not assigned to Groups 1, 2, or 3 of Executive Order No. 10501, as amended, shall be excluded from the General Declassification Schedule. However, at any time after the expiration of ten years from the date of origin it shall be subject to a mandatory classification review and disposition under the same conditions and criteria that apply to classified information and material created after the effective date of this order as set forth in (B) and (C) above.

(E) *Declassification of Classified Information or Material After Thirty Years.* All classified information or material which is thirty years old or more, whether originating before or after the effective date of this order, shall be declassified under the following conditions:

(1) All information and material classified after the effective date of this order shall, whether or not declassification has been requested, become automatically declassified at the end of thirty full calendar years after the date of its original classification except for such specifically identified information or material which the head of the originating Department personally determines in writing at that time to require continued protection because such continued protection is essential to the national security or disclosure would place a person in immediate jeopardy. In such case, the head of the Department shall also specify the period of continued classification.

(2) All information and material classified before the effective date of this order and more than thirty years old shall be systematically reviewed for declassification by the Archivist of the United States by the end of the thirtieth full calendar year following the year in which it was originated. In his review, the Archivist will separate and keep protected only such information or material as is specifically identified by the head of the Department in accordance with (E)(1) above. In such case, the head of the Department shall also specify the period of continued classification.

(F) *Departments Which Do Not Have Authority For Original Classification.* The provisions of this section relating to the declassification of national security information or material shall apply to Departments which, under the terms of this order, do not have current authority to originally classify information or material, but which formerly had such authority under previous Executive orders.

Section 6. Policy Directives on Access, Marking, Safekeeping, Accountability, Transmission, Disposition and Destruction of Classified Information and Material. The President acting through the National Security Council shall issue directives which shall be binding on all Departments to protect classified information from loss or compromise. Such directives shall conform to the following policies:

(A) No person shall be given access to classified information or material unless such person has been determined to be trustworthy and unless access to such information is necessary for the performance of his duties.

(B) All classified information and material shall be appropriately and conspicuously marked to put all persons on clear notice of its classified contents.

(C) Classified information and material shall be used, possessed, and stored only under conditions which will prevent access by unauthorized persons or dissemination to unauthorized persons.

(D) All classified information and material disseminated outside the executive branch under Executive Order No. 10865 or otherwise shall be properly protected.

(E) Appropriate accountability records for classified information shall be established and maintained and such information and material shall be protected adequately during all transmissions.

(F) Classified information and material no longer needed in current working files or for reference or record purposes shall be destroyed or disposed of in accordance with the records disposal provisions contained in Chapter 33 of Title 44 of the United States Code and other applicable statutes.

(G) Classified information or material shall be reviewed on a systematic basis for the purpose of accomplishing downgrading, declassification, transfer, retirement and destruction at the earliest practicable date.

Section 7. Implementation and Review Responsibilities.

(A) The National Security Council shall monitor the implementation of this order. To assist the National Security Council, an Interagency Classification Review Committee shall be established, composed of representatives of the Departments of State, Defense and Justice, the Atomic Energy Commission, the Central Intelligence Agency and the National Security Council Staff and a Chairman designated by the President. Representatives of other Departments in the executive branch may be invited to meet with the Committee on matters of particular interest to those Departments. This Committee shall meet regularly and on a continuing basis shall review and take action to ensure compliance with this order, and in particular:

(1) The Committee shall oversee Department actions to ensure compliance with the provisions of this order and implementing directives issued by the President through the National Security Council.

(2) The Committee shall, subject to procedures to be established by it, receive, consider and take action on suggestions and complaints from persons within or without the government with respect to the administration of this order, and in consultation with the affected Department or Departments assure that appropriate action is taken on such suggestions and complaints.

(3) Upon request of the Committee Chairman, any Department shall furnish to the Committee any particular information or material needed by the Committee in carrying out its functions.

(B) To promote the basic purposes of this order, the head of each Department originating or handling classified information or material shall:

(1) Prior to the effective date of this order submit to the Interagency Classification Review Committee for approval a copy of the regulations it proposes to adopt pursuant to this order.

(2) Designate a senior member of his staff who shall ensure effective compliance with and implementation of this order and shall also chair a Departmental committee which shall have authority to act on all suggestions and complaints with respect to the Department's administration of this order.

(3) Undertake an initial program to familiarize the employees of his Department with the provisions of this order. He shall also establish and maintain active training and orientation programs for employees concerned with classified information or material. Such programs shall include, as a minimum, the briefing of new employees and periodic reorientation during employment to impress upon each individual his responsibility for exercising vigilance and care in complying with the provisions of this order. Additionally, upon termination of employment or contemplated temporary separation for a sixty-day period or more, employees shall be debriefed and each reminded of the provisions of the Criminal Code and other applicable provisions of law relating to penalties for unauthorized disclosure.

(C) The Attorney General, upon request of the head of a Department, his duly designated representative, or the Chairman of the above described Committee, shall personally or through authorized representatives of the Department of Justice render an interpretation of this order with respect to any question arising in the course of its administration.

Section 8. Material Covered by the Atomic Energy Act. Nothing in this order shall supersede any requirements made by or under the Atomic Energy Act of August 30, 1954, as amended. "Restricted Data," and material designated as "Formerly Restricted Data," shall be handled, protected, classified, downgraded and declassified in conformity with the provisions of the Atomic Energy Act of 1954, as amended, and the regulations of the Atomic Energy Commission.

Section 9. Special Departmental Arrangements. The originating Department or other appropriate authority may impose, in conformity with the provisions of this order, special requirements with respect to access, distribution and protection of classified information and material, including those which presently relate to communications intelligence, intelligence sources and methods and cryptography.

Section 10. Exceptional Cases. In an exceptional case when a person or Department not authorized to classify information originates information which is believed to require classification, such person or Department shall protect that information in the manner prescribed by this order. Such persons or Department shall transmit the information forthwith, under appropriate safeguards, to the Department having primary interest in the subject matter with a request that a determination be made as to classification.

Section 11. Declassification of Presidential Papers. The Archivist of the United States shall have authority to review and declassify information and material which has been classified by a President, his White House Staff or special committee or commission appointed by him and which the Archivist has in his custody at any archival depository, including a Presidential Library. Such declassification shall only be undertaken in accord with: (i) the terms of the donor's deed of gift, (ii) consultations with Departments having a primary subject-matter interest, and (iii) the provisions of Section 5.

Section 12. Historical Research and Access by Former Government Officials. The requirement in Section 6(A) that access to classified information or material be granted only as is necessary for the performance of one's duties shall not apply to persons outside the executive branch who are engaged in historical research projects or who have previously occupied policy-making positions to which they were appointed by the President; *Provided,* however, that in each case the head of the originating Department shall:

> (i)   determine that access is clearly consistent with the interests of national security; and
>
> (ii)   take appropriate steps to assure that classified information or material is not published or otherwise compromised.

Access granted a person by reason of his having previously occupied a policy-making position shall be limited to those papers which the former official originated, reviewed, signed or received while in public office.

Section 13. Administrative and Judicial Action.

(A)   Any officer or employee of the United States who unnecessarily classifies or over-classifies information or material shall be notified that his actions are in violation of the terms of this order or of a directive of the President issued through the National Security Council. Repeated abuse of the classification process shall be grounds for an administrative reprimand. In any case where the Departmental committee or the Interagency Classification Review Committee finds that unnecessary classification or over-classification has occurred, it shall make a report to the head of the Department concerned in order that corrective steps may be taken.

(B)   The head of each Department is directed to take prompt and stringent administrative action against any officer or employee of the United States, at any level of employment, determined to have been responsible for any release or disclosure of national security information or material in a manner not authorized by or under this order or a directive of the President issued through the National Security Council. Where a violation of criminal statutes may be involved, Departments will refer any such case promptly to the Department of Justice.

Section 14. Revocation of Executive Order No. 10501. Executive Order No. 10501 of November 5, 1953, as amended by Executive Orders No. 10816 of May 8, 1959, No. 10901 of January 11, 1961, No. 10964 of September 20, 1961, No. 10985 of January 15, 1962, No. 11097 of March 6, 1963 and by Section 1(a) of No. 11382 of November 28, 1967, are superseded as of the effective date of this order.

Section 15. Effective Date. This order shall become effective on June 1, 1972.

RICHARD NIXON

THE WHITE HOUSE,
    March 8, 1972

Appendix 3

Letter from former Secretary of State Dean Acheson

September 1, 1971

Dear Mr. Fox:

The Special Delivery letter slips easily through the door slot, but the messenger is not concerned with signs of habitation. So your letter waited a week or more for discovery.

You ask my views of the security classification system, which you have been "researching" since January. Too often research means turning over the documentary manure in departmental barnyards rather than preparing the seeds of thought one wishes to fertilize. The issue often is made to be between the bureaucrats' desire for protective secrecy and the public's and scholar's need and right to know. Neither, I think, are valid interests in a broad sense, but I shall return to them as well as to the preference given to former officials in preparing memoirs. These are all of secondary importance.

Government officers in nearly all fields need protection from publicity and outside (public) interference in studying, discussing, and making decisions on most matters, certainly at early stages. This is clear in diplomacy and defense. It is also true in NIH decisions on priorities in medical research and the same in Agriculture on the study of pests. Indeed, in most work—governmental, business, and professional—the importance of privacy outweighs the contribution of over-the-shoulder kibitzing. . .

So I would say to the researcher, get your values straight before you start and, in doing so, don't believe all you read, hear, and see about the need for a democratic system to know all, see all, and have a cloud of witnesses participate in all to report it daily. I would reverse most folk beliefs in this field.

Furthermore, the incredible multiplicity and fecundity of record communication devices make person-to-person communication nearly impossible. The XYZ papers nearly involved the United States in war with France and they were handwritten and published by the government. Today the *New York Times* would have had them before they were dispatched. When in 1949 we negotiated the end of the blockade of Berlin only five persons in the United States knew the matter was under discussion and, as I recall, no written record was made until agreement was ready for release. It is hard for me to believe that arrangements for Mr. Kissinger's journey to Peking could have been made through any agency in the United States.

There are thus some matters regarding which privacy, often amounting to complete secrecy, is desirable or essential. For these, high classifications and stiff official-secrets-act penalties are necessary, though some I would not trust to paper at all and would share with very few people. Some of these papers—or, at least, their substance—need remain secret only for a fairly short time, until, for instance, the Berlin agreement and Council of Foreign Ministers Meeting of 1949 was announced.

Other papers require to remain closed for varying lengths of time and to have varying security classifications. Generally speaking I would reach some gentlemen's agreement on a closed period for communications between foreign statesmen to encourage candid discussion. Twenty-five years does not seem excessive unless earlier consent is given. Where it seemed necessary to get out a White Paper that might be harmful to foreign diplomatic personnel, editing might be necessary.

As I look back over my own experience in public office, I am impressed by two factors bearing on the time the general run of papers should be closed to public examination. One is the period after which there is little danger the disclosure of these papers would impair the public interest. The other is the longer period when the sensation monger—politician, journalist, or self-styled scholar—would be tempted to embarrass a public official by something he had written under different circumstances. The former I would put at about ten years; the latter at, say, fifteen. I don't mind particularly people being embarrassed in later life; but I should regret their being cagey and over-cautious when young. The classification of the highest secrets should be reviewed after fifteen years.

In sum, this is a hard problem and not as important as articulate liberals would make it appear. The scholarly victims of the "publish or perish" doctrine don't warrant much concern. It is easier to modify the system that pinches them. . . . As for former officials as memoir writers, they have something special to offer, as many historians have told me. The why of many events, the decisive why, is apt to survive only in their memory. The use of documents to me was most important more as a corrective to memory than as a supplement. My memory, I find, is often very clear and at the same time mixed up, sometimes putting people at places and meetings at which they were not present or as taking positions taken by others. The memoranda taken at the time straighten out a sometimes involved sequence. Furthermore, an active imagination or twice-told tale often creates the equivalent of Sam Morison's "Flyaway Islands," which bedeviled the early cartographers. If it isn't in the record, the memoir-writer should doubt it.

Sincerely yours,

Dean Acheson

Appendix 4

Letter from former Secretary of State Dean Rusk

August 24, 1971

Dear Mr. Fox:

The questions you posed in your letter of August 20 would require a volume in reply. What follows is simply an oversimplified digest of my reactions; if you wish to explore one or another question more fully, please write me again.

I agree that the present 25-year embargo in the State Department is too long. As a matter of policy, the period is 20 years; the difference between the two figures turns upon budget and staff and these are influenced by the enormous increase in international business which now requires 8-10 volumes per year in the *Foreign Relations* series. I am glad to learn that Dr. Franklin is hopeful of getting additional staff in which to move the 25 years down towards the 20 years.

As you perhaps know, I take a rather poor view of books written by high officials of government shortly after they leave office. They are frequently self serving, sometimes reveal discussions with other governments which ought to remain private for a longer period, and are not subject to the hard hitting criticism by scholars and historians with full access to the material. I exempt from my statement those books written by former Presidents; I happen to think that they are in a special category. I also did not object to Dean Acheson's *Present at the Creation* because he at least waited 17 years and did not fill his footnotes with references for materials which are not available to other people. One of my problems with the Pentagon Papers is that they are extracted from tons and tons of materials and the fair and impartial scholar has no basis on which he can make a responsible judgment.

On your specific point as to whether former officials and privileged writers should be given access which is denied to others, I am inclined to think that former officials should have access to those materials which related directly to their own particular position in public life but the declassification of materials in their case should be subject to the same criteria which apply to the general process of declassification. I do not know who you mean by "privileged writers" but I am pretty skeptical about extending such privileges on a selective basis.

My primary concern about secrecy for a reasonable period is pretty well concentrated on the necessity for preserving the ability of the United States Government to talk privately with high officials of other governments. Public debate and public diplomacy just cannot resolve the many problems which arise in the normal course of international affairs. The very process of negotiation requires privacy if it is not to degenerate into a public harangue. Privately, ideas can be tried out tentatively, a greater degree of frankness can be used in assessing one's own or one's opponent's point of view, compromises and adjustments can be more readily achieved. Many an agreement has elements which are both agreeable and disagreeable to the peoples of the respective sides. When the whole package is viewed, both sides might find enough benefit in which to be able to proceed. If the negotiation were public, however, it would be very difficult to make adjustments which might inflame the public opinion of either side, one's allies or one's adversaries. When I announced in the mid-1960's that I would not write my memoirs, quite a number of foreign ministers spoke to me about it and said that they thought it was a very good idea.

I have no doubt that there is considerable over-classification in government, although I know of no society in the world in which our public business is more exposed to public view than is the case in the United States. In theory, we could declassify a great deal of material more rapidly than is now done, although that would take large staffs and substantial appropriations. But there is a difficulty; by declassifying rapidly, say 80% of the material on a given subject, the 20% which remains classified might be crucial in making a fair judgment about the 80%. I must confess, therefore, that I am strongly prejudiced towards the notion of general declassification after 20 years rather than piecemeal declassification based upon the sensitivity of particular documents.

You repeat your question about former government officials. I might add that I think that former government officials ought to be allowed to see classified documents to assist them in recalling what they did and what they had in mind in particular situations, but that the documents themselves should not be declassified except under general criteria.

Your reference to "objective history based on complete documentation" stimulates another remark. I doubt that there is very much objective history or that there are very many objective historians. Free press, free speech, and free scholarship are not based upon the notion that those involved will tell the "truth"—whatever that is. The idea is that, if everyone is free to say and write what he likes, truth has a better chance to emerge than if these processes were subject to control. I am interested in the contest of views and conflicting opinions which would emerge out of "complete documentation". I must say that I despair for the future historian when I reflect upon the blizzard of paper which has fallen in upon us. The sheer mass of the written record will make it almost impossible for historians to write accurately and in full context about the history of the period, say, since World War II. This is a problem in historiography which requires much more attention than it has had and maybe the Twentieth Century Fund can think of some new ways to get at it. While I was Secretary of State, two million, one hundred thousand cables went out of the Department of State. I doubt that any single historian will be able to see as many as 1% of them—because the historian, too, is mortal and can't live forever.

Sincerely yours,

Dean Rusk

Bibliography

A. Books

Acheson, Dean. *Present at the Creation: My Years in the State Department.* New York, The New American Library, 1970.

Dallin, David J. *Soviet Espionage.* New Haven, Yale University Press, 1955.

Draper, Theodore. *The Dominican Revolt: A Case Study in American Policy.* New York, Commentary, 1968.

Fairbank, John King. *The United States and China.* New York, The Viking Press, 1962.

Feis, Herbert. *The China Tangle.* Princeton, Princeton University Press, 1953.

Johnson, Lyndon Baines. *The Vantage Point: Perspectives of the Presidency 1963–1969.* New York, Holt, Rinehart and Winston, 1971.

Kennedy, Robert F. *Thirteen Days: A Memoir of the Cuban Missile Crisis.* New York, W. W. Norton & Company, Inc., 1969.

Ladd, Bruce. *Crisis in Credibility.* New York, The New American Library, 1968.

Latham, Earl. *The Communist Controversy in Washington: From the New Deal to McCarthy.* Cambridge, Harvard University Press, 1966.

Loewenheim, Francis L., ed. *The Historian and the Diplomat.* New York, Harper & Row, 1966.

Reedy, George E. *The Twilight of the Presidency.* New York, The World Publishing Company, 1970.

Rourke, Francis E. *Secrecy and Publicity: Dilemmas of Democracy.* Baltimore, Johns Hopkins Press, 1961.

Rundell, Walter, Jr. *In Pursuit of American History: Research and Training in the United States.* Norman, University of Oklahoma Press, 1970.

Shewmaker, Kenneth E. *Americans and Chinese Communists, 1927-1945: A Persuading Encounter.* Ithaca, Cornell University Press, 1971.

Slater, Jerome. *Intervention and Negotiation: The United States and the Dominican Revolution.* New York, Harper & Row, 1970.

The New York Times, ed. *The Pentagon Papers as published by The New York Times.* New York, Bantam Books, 1971.

Tsou, Tang. *America's Failure in China, 1941-50,* Volumes I and II. Chicago, University of Chicago Press, 1967.

U.S., Department of State. *China White Paper: August 1941,* reissued with a new introduction by Lyman P. Van Slyke. Stanford, Stanford University Press, 1970.

Wiggins, James Russell. *Freedom or Secrecy.* Revised ed. New York, Oxford University Press, 1964.

B. Articles

Berle, Adolf A. and Malcolm Moos. "The Need to Know and the Right to Tell: Emmet John Hughes, *The Ordeal of Power*—A Discussion," *Political Science Quarterly* 79, no. 2 (June 1964), pp. 161-83.

Burns, James MacGregor. "The Historian's Right to See," *The New York Times Book Review* (November 8, 1970), pp. 2, 42-44.

Commager, Henry Steele. "Should Historians Write Contemporary History?" *Saturday Review* (February 12, 1966), pp. 18-20, 47.

Davis, Kenneth Culp. "The Information Act: A Preliminary Analysis," *The University of Chicago Law Review* 34 (1967), pp. 761-816.

De Conde, Alexander. "What's Wrong with American Diplomatic History," *SHAFR Newsletter* (Society for Historians of American Foreign Relations) 1, no. 2 (May 1970), pp. 1-16.

Diamond, Edwin. "The Johnson Version," *New York* (September 28, 1970), pp. 38-45.

Draper, Theodore. "The Dominican Intervention Reconsidered," *Political Science Quarterly* 86, no. 1 (March 1971), pp. 1-36.

Feis, Herbert. "The President's Making of History," *Atlantic Monthly* (September 1969), pp. 64-65.

————. "The Shackled Historian," *Foreign Affairs* 45 (January 1967), pp. 332-43.

————. "Unpublic Public Papers," *The New York Times Book Review* (April 21, 1968), pp. 2, 58.

Frankel, Max. "The 'State Secrets' Myth," *Columbia Journalism Review* (September/October 1971), pp. 22-26.

Franklin, William M. "The Future of the 'Foreign Relations' Series," *Department of State Bulletin* 61, no. 1577 (September 15, 1969), pp. 247-56.

Kahn, Herman. "Comments on 'The Historian and the Federal Government'," *Prologue: The Journal of the American Archives* 3, no. 1 (Spring 1971), pp. 12-14.

Katz, Joan M. "The Games Bureaucrats Play: Hide and Seek Under the Freedom of Information Act," *The Texas Law Review* 48 (1970), pp. 1261-84.

Langer, William L. "The Historian's Right to See," Letter to the Editor, *The New York Times Book Review* (December 14, 1970), p. 12.

Leopold, Richard W. "A Crisis of Confidence: Foreign Policy Research and the Federal Government," *American Archivist* 34, no. 2 (April 1971), pp. 139-55.

————. "The *Foreign Relations* Series: A Centennial Estimate," *The Mississippi Valley Historical Review* 49, no. 4 (March 1963), pp. 595-612.

May, Ernest R. "A Case for 'Court Historians'," *Perspectives in American History* 3 (1969), pp. 413-32.

McCartney, James. "What Should Be Secret?" *Columbia Journalism Review* (September/October 1971), pp. 40-44.

Morton, Louis. "The Historian and the Federal Government: A Proposal for a Government-Wide Historical Office," *Prologue: The Journal of the National Archives* 3, no. 1 (Spring 1971), pp. 3-11.

Moynihan, Daniel P. "The Presidency and the Press," *Commentary* 50 (March 1971), pp. 41-52.

Roche, John P. "The Jigsaw Puzzle of History," *The New York Times Magazine* (January 24, 1971), pp. 14-15, 35-44.

Rothchild, John H. "Finding the Facts Bureaucrats Hide," *The Washington Monthly* 3, no. 11 (January 1972), pp. 15-27.

Rundell, Walter, Jr. "Uncle Sam the Historian: Federal Historical Activities," *The Historian* 33 (November 1970), pp. 1-20.

Schlesinger, Arthur, Jr. "Eyeless in Indochina," *The New York Review of Books* 17, no. 6 (October 21, 1971), pp. 23-32.

―――. "The Historian and History," *Foreign Affairs* 41, no. 3 (April 1963), pp. 491-97.

―――. "The Historian as Participant," *Daedelus* 100, no. 2 (Spring 1971), pp. 339-58.

―――. "The Secrecy Dilemma," *The New York Times Magazine* (February 6, 1972), pp. 12-13, 38-50.

Sheppard, William F. "The Plight of 'Foreign Relations': A Plea for Action," *AHA Newsletter* 9, no. 5 (November 1971), pp. 22-27.

Ullman, Richard H. "The Pentagon's History as 'History'," *Foreign Policy* 4 (Fall 1971), pp. 150-55.

Weisberger, Bernard. "The Paper Trust," *American Heritage* 12, no. 3 (April 1971), pp. 38-41, 104-7.

Wiarda, Howard J. "The Dominican Revolution in Perspective: A Research Note," *Polity* 1, no. 1 (Fall 1968), pp. 114-24.

Wicker, Tom. "The Greening of the Press," *Columbia Journalism Review* (May/June 1971), pp. 7-12.

C. Official Sources

U.S., Congress, House, Committee on Government Operations. *Freedom of Information Act (Compilation and Analysis of Departmental Regulations Implementing 5 U.S.C. 552).* 90th Cong., 2d. sess., 1968.

U.S., Congress, House, Committee on Government Operations. *To Provide for the Acceptance and Maintenance of Presidential Libraries, and for Other Purposes: Hearings on H. J. Res. 330, H. J. Res. 331, H. J. Res. 332.* 84th Cong., 1st sess., 1955.

U.S., Congress, House, Committee on Government Operations. *U.S. Government Information Policies and Practices—The Pentagon Papers.* 92nd Cong., 1st sess., 1971.

U.S., Congress, Senate, Committee on Foreign Relations. *Security Agreements and Commitments Abroad.* 91st Cong., 2nd sess., 1970.

U.S., Department of Justice. *Attorney General's Memorandum on the Public Information Section of the Administrative Procedure Act.* June 1967.

D. Unpublished Sources

Final Report of the Joint AHA-OAH Ad Hoc Committee to Investigate the Charges Against the Franklin D. Roosevelt Library and Related Matters. August 24, 1970.

May, Ernest R. "A Twenty-Year Rule," paper read at the American Historical Association annual meeting, December 30, 1971, in New York. Mimeographed.

"Reply by the National Archives and Record Service, General Services Administration, to the Final Report of the Joint AHA-OAH *Ad Hoc* Committee to Investigate the Charges Against the Franklin D. Roosevelt Library and Related Matters, August 24, 1970," November 19, 1970. Mimeographed.